THE KURDISH REVOLT

THE KURDISH REVOLT:
1961–1970

EDGAR O'BALLANCE

ARCHON BOOKS

1973

Library of Congress Cataloging in Publication Data

O'Ballance, Edgar.
  The Kurdish revolt: 1961–1970.

  Bibliography: p.
  1. Kurds in Iraq. 2. Iraq—Politics and government. I. Title.
DS51.K7022   1973   956.7'04   73–5817
ISBN 0–208–01395–4

First published in 1973
by Faber and Faber Limited, London,
and in the United States of America
as an Archon Book by
The Shoe String Press, Inc.,
Hamden, Connecticut 06514
All rights reserved

Printed in Great Britain

CONTENTS

7

Acknowledgements

This work has been compiled mainly from notes I made when touring Kurdish territory and interviewing prominent personalities, both Arab Iraqis and Kurds, and seeing something of the Iraqi armed forces and the Pesh Merga at first hand, together with my own practical researches, observations and other interviews, but I would like to record that I have read with interest, profit and pleasure the following works, and I wish to make grateful acknowledgement to the authors, editors or compilers of them.

Adamson, David, *The Kurdish War*, Allen & Unwin (1964).

Arfa, Hassan, *The Kurds*, Oxford University Press (1966).

Avery, Peter, *Modern Iran*, Benn (1965).

Brown, J. Gilbert, *The Iraq Levies*, Royal United Service Institution Publication (1932).

Dann, Uriel, *Iraq under Kassem*, Praeger (New York) (1969).

Ghassemlou, Abdul Rahman, *Kurdistan and the Kurds*, Collets (London) (1965).

Mauries, René, *Le Kurdistan ou le Mort*, Robert Laffont (1967).

Schmidt, Dana Adams, *Journey among Brave Men*, Little Brown (Boston, USA) (1964).

Preface

Perhaps the Kurds are destined always to be a race and never a nation. Less than a century ago they were still a collection of wild tribes, some migratory, some aggressive and mutually hostile, with no national cohesion and bound together only by the loose bonds of language, culture and tribal customs. Living for 4,000 years in an inland mountainous region, near where Asia joins Europe in the Middle East, they remained a turbulent people. No trace of political nationalism emerged until 1880, when Sheikh Ubeidullah tried unsuccessfully to detach a part of Persian territory to make it an autonomous Kurdish satellite of the decaying Ottoman Empire. Nationalism developed extremely slowly, so the Kurds were not ready to take full political advantage of the chaos of World War I and its aftermath. The Turkish Empire was dismantled and a fresh map drawn of the Middle East that included newly emergent states, but no independent Kurdish nation was established. In the 1920s Kurdish insurrections in Turkey and Persia were put down firmly by the authorities, until Persia was able to declare that it 'had no Kurdish Problem', while Turkey went one better by refusing to admit that it had any Kurds at all, only 'mountain Turks who had forgotten their native tongue'. Despite a weak régime and weak military forces, the Kurds in Iraq were also subdued, at least overtly, by 1935, but circumstances compelled the Government to leave them much to their own devices in the mountains.

The story of the nine-year Kurdish Revolt, which was confined entirely to Iraq, begins in 1943, and is largely, but not completely, the story of one man, Mullah Mustafa Barzani. Although, naturally, many other personalities were involved, he became the acknowledged leader who inspired the Revolt and dominated it throughout. He and his tribe of warring Barzanis, feared and hated by other Kurdish tribes, were the mainstay of the unfortunate Kurdish Republic of Mahabad, precariously established on Persian territory in 1946. It suddenly collapsed, after a lack-lustre existence of slightly less than one year, when Soviet occupation troops were withdrawn

11

from Persia, allowing Persian soldiers to march against it. A fighting escape into Iraq by Mullah Mustafa and his Barzanis was followed by an epic fighting retreat across the mountains until he found refuge in the Soviet Union, where he remained for eleven years. When Kassem came to power in 1958, Mullah Mustafa was allowed to return to Iraq on the condition that he became Chairman of the United Democratic Party of Kurdistan. It was only in 1961 when he realized that Kassem was not going to grant any of the Kurdish political demands that he took to the mountains.

The pattern of the military operations in the Revolt was the old constantly repeated story: the Kurds could hold out in, or retreat farther into, the mountains in the face of attacks and pressure from conventional Government forces, but were unable to counter-attack successfully down on to the plains of Iraq, while the Iraqi army, with nearly 600 tanks, was strong on the plains but comparatively ineffectual and vulnerable when it attempted to penetrate into the mountains, which terrain, with few tracks and hardly any motorable roads, was ideal for partisan-type warfare. Repeated Government military offensives, while hurting the Kurds, were almost always abortive, and maintaining or combating them sapped the strength of both sides, causing periods of prolonged inactivity; during these they issued boastful and wildly inaccurate communiqués, prompting months of sterile negotiations when Kurds and the Iraqi Government sat down to 'catch their breath' and to play for time. The Revolt underlined the lesson, still barely and reluctantly accepted by many, that while causing fear, casualties, hardship and a refugee problem, air power was not a decisive factor in this type of warfare, and that protracted resistance by a determined people can be put up without any at all.

No new lessons of warfare or new techniques of strategy or tactics were discovered or developed, but old-established ones were emphasized. Achievements seemed to be negative as neither side made any substantial or territorial gain after the first stalemate. A conclusion that may disappoint romantic sympathizers with the Kurdish cause is that the prospects of an independent Kurdistan, of any size or strength, emerging in the future, are poor. Of considerable interest to the student of Communist tactics was the persistent failure of the Politburo of the Democratic Party of Kurdistan, the DPK, practically all Communist in composition, to impose its leadership on the Revolt. If it had been able to exercise its superior organizational, political and military capabilities, the course of the Revolt might have been slightly different, but Mullah Mustafa outwitted it continually.

Prosperity and material advantages, limited as they are in Iraq and the Middle East generally, are the magnet that draws individual Kurds from their mountains in ever-increasing numbers to seek jobs that give them a far higher standard of living and comfort than they would ever have in their barren and inhospitable homeland. After having tasted them, they are reluctant to return to the shackles of tribal authority and customs. Involuntary depopulation is achieving to a degree what the Iraqi armed forces could not.

The Iraqi Government did its best to conceal the Kurdish Revolt from the eyes of the world, with perhaps understandable motives. In this it was frequently successful because the Revolt coincided with and was heavily overshadowed by other momentous events in the Middle East, such as Arab rivalries, the death of Kassem, the Third Arab–Israeli War, and indeed the Vietnam War farther afield. Kurdish propaganda aimed at overseas opinion was pathetically weak. This factor, essential to a revolution, was either overlooked completely or not appreciated. Press coverage, too, of events in Kurdish territory, was hampered by the governments of Iraq, Persia and Turkey. Consequently the Kurds gained no powerful adherents in Western countries who could have agitated on world platforms in their support. Almost until the end the Kurds fought silently, and therefore alone, their aspirations and struggles unknown. They developed an introversion, an inward-looking complex that was to their great detriment.

Both sides had their strengths and weaknesses, their victories and defeats; both lost opportunities and seized advantages. Holding no brief for either, I have related the story as an outsider, and unfolded the facts as they appear to me, and not necessarily as either the Kurds or the Iraqi Governments would like them to be shown.

The purist may occasionally raise an eyebrow at the spelling of Arab and other names. In the interests of the general reader, I have adopted accepted Western forms.

EDGAR O'BALLANCE

1

THE KURDS

'There the Greeks spent a happy night, with plenty to eat, talking about the struggle now past. For they had been seven days passing through the country of the Kurds, fighting all the time, and they had suffered worse things at the hands of the Kurds than all that the King of Persia, and his general, Tissaphernes, could do to them.'

Anabasis of Xenophon (400 B.C.)

The Kurdish tribes which inhabit the sprawling mountainous sector of territory lying amid the Middle East land mass that is roughly encompassed by the Black Sea, the Caspian Sea, the Persian Gulf and the Mediterranean, claim that they have lived there for over 4,000 years and that they are of Aryan stock, probably descended from the Medes, who gained classical fame in ancient chronicles for their struggles against the Persians. Sturdy, warlike and of independent character, over the centuries they have never been assimilated by successive conquerors. Perhaps the Kurd in history best known to Western readers was Sala ad-Din al-Ayubi, Saladin of the Crusades, born at Takrit[1] on the River Tigris in 1137, who fought against Richard Coeur de Lion and forced the Crusaders to abandon practically all Palestine except for a few coastal forts. Another fact of Western interest is that Mount Ararat (in present-day Turkey), where, according to biblical tradition, the Ark of Noah came to rest after the subsidence of the Flood, lies in Kurdish territory.

The Kurds, as a collective name, was given to these wild tribes by the conquering and evangelizing Arabs in the 7th century, who converted them forcibly to Mohammedanism, and then abruptly left them alone in their mountain fastnesses. During the 13th century the Mongols subdued adjacent areas, but hesitated to penetrate the Kurdish mountains, and it was not until the end of the following century that Amir Timur (Tamerlane) succeeded in bringing the Kurdish tribes under firm control, in his customary barbaric manner. There was never Kurdish unity or national cohesion as such; in the Middle Ages the tribes were grouped into about thirty mutually

[1] In present-day Iraq.

15

hostile principalities. Wedged in between the rival, expanding empires of Persia and Turkey, some fought for one side and some for the other, depending upon pressures, bribes and circumstances, and more frequently against each other.

In 1639 the Turks and Persians made a treaty demarcating a common frontier which cut practically straight through Kurdish territory, thus nominally dividing it into two parts, but with the decline of the two empires few attempts were made to penetrate and pacify these areas, apart from the occasional punitive expedition, which usually had limited objectives. The several princes (atabegs, or tribal sheikhs) remained autonomous within their own small localities, and the whole region became a sort of wild tribal 'no man's land', remote and impenetrable, a convenient geographical and political mountainous buffer. During the early 19th century Persian and Ottoman overlordship remained nominal; both used Kurdish irregulars in their wars with each other, and against Russia, but from the mid-century onwards, as the Ottoman administration became more centralized and stronger, Turkish authority over the Kurds increased.

There was still no sign that the tribes were becoming fused into a nation; they remained a restless mass, one forever attempting to dominate the other, resisting attempts to bring them under either Turkish or Persian authority. The first sign of Kurdish political nationalism occurred in 1880, when a Kurdish sheikh named Ubeidullah, who lived in what was nominally Turkish territory, invaded the Kurdish region, nominally controlled by Persia, with the object of bringing into being a Kurdish national state which would owe allegiance to Turkey. He was given some support by the Turkish Sultan, who visualized adding another slice of territory to the Ottoman Empire at the expense of his old enemies, the Persians. Sheikh Ubeidullah managed to rally a number of tribes to his banner and persuade several thousand warriors to join in his eastwards offensive, his official reason and excuse being to take revenge for alleged attacks on Persian Kurds by Government forces. He halted in the mountains overlooking the town of Rezaieh, just to the west of Lake Rezaieh,[1] on the shore of which lived a community of Assyrian Nestorians, one of the few left in the world. The Nestorians[2] were all expecting to

---

[1] Formerly Lake Urmia.

[2] The Nestorians were descendants of the followers of the heretical Nestorius, a 5th-century Patriarch of Constantinople, who insisted that Christ was two persons, one human and the other divine, and that the Virgin Mary was the

be killed, but they were saved by an American missionary, who was with them at the time. This missionary knew Sheikh Ubeidullah and was reputed to have cured his wife of an illness. Knowing that a Persian relief force had been mustered and would soon arrive, he persuaded the Sheikh to postpone his attack for a few days. Then, as the Persian force approached, Sheikh Ubeidullah's followers began to fade away, and he was forced to withdraw quickly into Turkey again. The unsuccessful Sheikh Ubeidullah was probably the first Kurdish nationalist leader of any note in modern history; he eventually died in exile in Mecca.

During the latter part of the 19th century Persia had no centrally controlled army, the only regular troops being the Royal Bodyguard and small garrisons to defend certain towns. A sort of tribal militia, or levy, raised to police the countryside, could be mustered for defence or punitive operations whenever necessary. The Persians were impressed by the Russian use of irregular Cossack cavalry to control the wilder and more remote regions of Russia, and they raised a standing force on similar lines, called the Cossack Force, in 1878. Its size varied, and many Kurds served in its ranks. The Turks also liked the idea, and in 1891 they raised some irregular Kurdish cavalry units, known as Hamidiye Regiments, which were mainly used to police the restless Kurds under their nominal control, and also to curb and deter the sometimes aggressive groups of Armenians and Assyrians who, often interspersed with Turks and Kurds, lived in Anatolia. During the Young Turks Revolution in 1908, a Kurdish sheikh with about 1,500 Kurdish irregulars occupied, and held, Damascus for the Sultan.

The Hamidiye Regiments remained loyal to the Sultan during World War I, despite Russian attempts to subvert them, and at one stage there were some thirty units of Kurdish irregular cavalry fighting on the Turkish eastern front. Russian troops were already in northern Persia when the war broke out in 1914, occupying Azerbaijan province, and as the Turks advanced towards them a 'war by proxy' commenced with Turkish Kurds fighting their old enemies, the Christian Armenians—now supported by Holy Russia—and also the Christian Assyrians. The Russians gave arms to the Armenians

---

mother of the human Christ. This was simply one of the many controversies that split the then rival Roman and Byzantine worlds.

Kurdish Territory

and recruited units of them. As arms were also smuggled to Kurds from various sources, the result was that there were many violent clashes between Kurds and Armenians, some of which on occasions amounted to mini-massacres. When the Russians invaded the Caucasus regions and moved into Kurdish tribal territory, they were preceded by groups of Armenian irregulars who killed and looted as they advanced; it was alleged that 'more than 600,000 Kurds (were) killed between 1915 and 1918 in the eastern vilayets of Turkey'.[1]

The Moslem Turks moved some 700,000 Christian Armenians from their homes to more southerly provinces to be away from possible Russian influence; many died of starvation or were killed by Kurds or Arabs. Accordingly, not only were large areas depopulated completely, but by the end of the war Armenians, and indeed Assyrians too, had practically disappeared from sectors they formerly occupied. The Russians had tried to implant thoughts of independence in the minds of both Kurds and Armenians, and these attempts probably gave the first authentic colour to the still embryonic, but uncertain, theory of a Kurdish nation, although a mild Kurdish nationalist organization had existed in Turkey since 1909.

British forces also advanced through the Middle East, and in May 1918 briefly occupied the town of Kirkuk, where they set up a local Kurdish administration. When they evacuated Kirkuk a few weeks later, the Turks reoccupied the town and dealt harshly with the Kurdish collaborators. The local Kurds resented being abandoned by the British, and the Turks had little difficulty in raising Kurdish irregulars to fight against them in that region.

Persia did not formally enter World War I. Because of its military weakness—it had only the Cossack Force and an armed gendarmerie, the latter raised as recently as 1911—Persia was compelled to remain passive while parts of its territory were devastated in turn by Turks, Russians, Kurds and Assyrians. In fact, since the 1907 Revolution, the Kurds in Persia had been virtually unfettered by authority; parts of Kurdish tribal territory had been occupied by the Turks in 1908, by the Russians in 1911, and again by the Russians in 1917. Persia had been in a state of political chaos since 1915 when, although the Shah had remained, most of the influential political personalities had hastily decamped from Teheran, the capital.

In 1914 the Assyrians, who lived mainly in the eastern parts of present-day Turkey and in some parts of Persia, declared war on

[1] *The Kurds* by Hassan Arfa, Oxford University Press (1966).

19

Turkey. They were hoping for Russian assistance, which was disappointingly sparse, and by 1917 they had been pushed first eastwards and then southwards into the Persian province of Azerbaijan, where they came up against Simko (Ismail Aka), Agha of the powerful Kurdish Shikak tribe, from east of Tabriz, who treacherously murdered the Mar Shimun, the Assyrian Patriarch, after shaking hands with him. With some Turkish help the Kurds were able to defeat a 6,000-strong avenging Assyrian force. Although the Assyrians took their revenge by killing many Kurds and others, as a nation they were virtually broken. Britain eventually allowed the remnants, some 40,000, to move into the newly created Kingdom of Iraq, to settle there.

The Kurds in Persia, who had already obtained extra arms, seized the chance to lay their hands on many more when, in 1917 and 1918, Russian soldiers revolted, killed their officers and withdrew into Russia. The situation in these regions deteriorated into complete anarchy; Kurds and Christians viciously attacked each other and Kurdish tribes squabbled among themselves. The only disciplined body in northern Persia was the Persian Cossack Force, which was far too small to be effective.

After World War I the Ottoman Empire was dismantled and new countries sprang into existence, which included Iraq (formed from the three former Turkish vilayets of Mosul, Baghdad and Basra), and Syria. This meant that instead of Kurdish territory spreading into only two countries, or three counting Russia, it now reached into five, that is Turkey, Persia, Iraq, Syria and what came eventually to be known as the Soviet Union. The spark of nationalism having been ignited and fanned, the Kurds anticipated that they would be granted autonomy under, they hoped, Turkish sovereignty, as most still looked in that direction for religious reasons if no other. Indeed, this was mentioned in the Treaty of Sèvres, of 1920, which stated that, 'A Commission . . . shall draft . . . a scheme for local autonomy for the predominantly Kurdish areas. . . .' But the Treaty of Lausanne, of 1923, did not confirm this. Other minorities, such as the Assyrians, also expected to be resettled and granted autonomy. The frontier between Turkey and Iraq was not demarcated for some time, and in particular the town of Mosul was a source of friction, both countries claiming it.

In May 1919 Sheikh Mahmoud Barzanji, a Kurd, who had been installed by the British as Governor of the town and district of

Suleimaniya, overcame the Government forces there and proclaimed its independence. The small British force sent against him was repulsed and a larger one, of divisional size, had to be dispatched, which captured the Sheikh. After this the area was comparatively quiet, although there remained a general atmosphere of hostility against the British. In the spring of 1922 some Turkish irregulars, who were Kurds, invaded territory claimed by Iraq, although the boundary was not yet decided and sectors were in dispute. They advanced towards Suleimaniya, which had been abandoned by the British, who released Sheikh Mahmoud Barzanji on condition that he would return and hold that town against the Turks for them. Instead, on arrival there, the Sheikh allied himself with the Turkish Kurds, and also with some Kurdish tribes in revolt against the Persian Government. In April 1923 elements of the newly-formed Iraqi Army, backed by the British-led Iraq levies and the RAF,[1] managed to reoccupy the town of Ruwandiz, which had been held by the Turkish irregulars. Next, this small force advanced and cleared Suleimaniya, but this town was evacuated again when the British, who had been granted the Mandate for Iraq, could not persuade any suitable local sheikh to become governor under their sponsorship.

However, Sheikh Mahmoud Barzanji, who had taken refuge in Persia, returned and came to an uneasy agreement with the Government to take charge once again in Suleimaniya in July 1923—but his good behaviour did not last long. Another military force had to be sent against him the following year (July 1924), when once again he fled to the Persian mountains; from there he attempted to wage partisan warfare with his Hamawand allies, a Kurdish tribe settled between Suleimaniya and Kirkuk. His raiding parties were occasionally bombed by RAF aircraft. In late 1926 the Sheikh again returned to Iraqi territory. Another military expedition was sent against him in March of the following year, when elements of the new Iraqi Army, with support from RAF bombers, drove him from his strongholds near Panjwin. Once more he retreated into Persia for refuge. However, by the summer of 1927 Persian military operations against the Kurds in Persia forced him back into Iraq, where he was arrested.

Another Kurdish trouble-maker for the Iraqi Government was Sheikh Ahmed, of Barzan, an area then completely without any governmental controls at all. A military force was dispatched which

[1] The RAF assumed responsibility for defence and internal security from the British Army in October 1922.

entered Barzan, a small town on the Greater Zab River, in June 1927, without meeting any resistance. A police post was established at Barzan, the centre of the turbulent Barzani tribe.

In 1926 a Tripartite Agreement between Britain, Turkey and Iraq fixed the common frontier between the two latter countries, and generally accepted the *de facto* demarcation line as the permanent border. This enabled both Turkey and Iraq to take steps to bring the Kurds in their respective territories under control. Mosul remained in Iraq.

In 1921, the embryo Iraqi Army was formed to be ultimately responsible for the defence of the country when the British Mandate was due to end (in 1931), and General Nuri el-Said, a former Turkish officer, an Iraqi, was made its first Chief of Staff. He had joined a revolutionary group at Basra early in World War I, been taken prisoner by the British, and recruited to join Sherif Hussein's desert revolt, in which he fought with Lawrence. The Iraqi Army relied upon voluntary recruitment, and by 1925[1] had a strength of some 7,500 men, at which level it remained until about 1933. Initially it consisted of six infantry battalions, three cavalry regiments, two mountain and one field battery, mainly formed into two field brigades; its officers had largely served in the old Turkish Army. A British Military Mission supervised its training, supplying instructors for its training centre and military college. Units of the new Iraqi Army took part in several operations against the Kurds. Meanwhile, the British military presence rapidly thinned out from thirty-five infantry battalions and other units in 1921 to three infantry battalions in 1926, the last of which left the country in 1928.

After the Mandate ended in 1932 there was talk of bringing in some form of conscription, which caused unrest, and when the National Service Law was passed in 1934 it was not immediately implemented. By 1933 the strength of the Iraqi Army had risen to about 11,500. As conscription was selectively introduced, it rose to about 23,000 by 1936. The country was divided into four territorial commands which, as more units were formed, developed into four infantry divisions.

Another small military force existed, known as the Iraq Levies, British-led and under the command of the British Air Officer Commanding in Iraq, which had developed from the handful of Arabs first enlisted by the British in 1915 and then known as the Arab

[1] *Iraq: 1900–1950* by Longrigg.

Scouts. Initially the personnel were all Arab, but when the Iraq Levies were expanded in 1921 to some 6,000 men they recruited Kurds, Assyrians, Turkomans and Yazidis as well. In 1922, for example, it was composed of three cavalry regiments (two Kurdish and one Assyrian), four infantry battalions (one Kurdish, two Assyrian and one of Marsh Arabs), and an Assyrian pack-battery.[1] The officers were British, Arab, Assyrian and Kurdish. The Iraq Levies were designed to fill the gap created by the departing British troops, until the new Iraqi Army was ready to assume full responsibility for the nation's defence. The Levies eventually settled down to a strength of about 7,500, and their personnel became predominantly Assyrian. They were frequently used on operations against the Kurds, when they were usually supported by the RAF.[2]

At first the Iraq Levies were used mainly to the south of Baghdad, but they had been gradually switched northwards to the troubled Kurdish areas, until by the late 1920s they were completely employed in such regions. Their early days were marked by a number of unfortunate occurrences. In particular the Assyrians,[3] who as Christians liked to consider themselves specially favoured by the British, behaved arrogantly towards the Moslems whenever they had the opportunity. For example, on one occasion, in May 1922, two Assyrian companies at Kirkuk mutinied and killed over fifty Moslems, and there were other unpleasant incidents. The some 40,000 Assyrians whom the British allowed into Iraq became a thorny problem; the British wanted to settle them in the country, but the proposal met stiff Arab and Kurdish opposition. Many were temporarily enlisted into the Iraq Levies until they could be resettled.

By 1928 the Kurdish question seemed to be slowly resolving itself from the point of view of the Government, which was anxious to unify the country. Hundreds of Kurds were serving in the Army, the police and in government administration at all levels, and a few were actually in the Government. The whole of the Kurdish territory in Iraq had been penetrated by government forces, and the mountain tribes seemed to be comparatively quiet and unaffected by Kurdish disturbances in neighbouring Turkey. This rather gave the impres-

[1] *Iraq: 1900-1950* by Longrigg
[2] According to Longrigg's *Iraq: 1900–1950*, the RAF strength in Iraq rose from four squadrons in 1921 to eight in 1926, and was reduced to five squadrons in 1928, and then four in 1930. The RAF worked mainly with the Iraq Levies.
[3] Reputed to have originally emigrated from Mesopotamia after the fall of Ur (about 2000 B.C.), the Assyrians spoke Syriac, the language of Christ.

sion that tribal discontent was subsiding and in any case had only been caused by outside agitation and ignorance, which would be gradually eliminated. Somehow it was overlooked that Kurdish nationalism was on the rise in Iraq, and when several Kurdish representatives in the Chamber of Deputies petitioned for Kurdish autonomy, they were brushed aside. The 1929 elections were boycotted by many Kurds, and there were protests, demonstrations and even riots in some Kurdish towns. These came as a surprise to the Government, which was faced with the fact that the Kurds expected some form of autonomy when the British Mandate ended.

Hoping to exploit the rising Kurdish nationalism, Sheikh Mahmoud Barzanji, who had once again escaped from house arrest, crossed the frontier in September 1930, rallied some Kurdish tribes in Persia and, loudly demanding an autonomous Kurdistan, invaded Iraq. The Iraqi Government mounted a military campaign against him, and drove him from the area of Panjwin, where he had established himself, but the Iraqi troops could neither encircle him nor drive him over the Persian border again before the winter snows set in. In March 1931 the Sheikh tried to raise the Kifri and Khanakin, Kurdish tribes that lived in the border region, but the Iraqi armed forces quickly stepped in and, after a sharp engagement near the village of Aui-Barika, succeeded in scattering the rebels, who fled leaving over twenty dead on the field of battle. Sheikh Mahmoud Barzanji again tried to escape into Persia, but was prevented by the Persian Army, then deployed in Kurdish territory along the border, so he returned to Panjwin to surrender. The Iraqi Government agreed to allow him to live under surveillance at Nasiriya.

From 1928 until the autumn of 1931 there had been an uneasy peace in the territory inhabited by the turbulent Barzani tribe, led by Sheikh Ahmed Barzani, an unstable character whose deviations from true Moslem practices caused the Sheikh of the adjacent, and rival, Baradosti tribe, to muster his tribesmen and march against him. Sheikh Ahmed retaliated and successfully advanced into Baradosti country, thus igniting inter-tribal warfare that grew to such proportions that Government troops had to be sent to the area. The Government force managed to penetrate as far as the town of Barzan, but was defeated near the town of Baradost and only saved from annihilation by RAF intervention. Punitive bombing forced Sheikh Ahmed to withdraw his Barzanis from Baradosti territory, but tribal squabbling continued to rumble on.

In the spring of 1932, before giving up the Mandate, the British tried to settle the remainder of the Assyrians who had been expelled from Turkey in the vicinity of Barzan. In violent protest, Sheikh Ahmed Barzani took to the field again with his warriors. Once again an Iraqi army column, with strong RAF support, managed to penetrate the mountains to occupy a large village, known as Margasur, where it was attacked by a force of Barzanis and heavily defeated. A month later another military operation was mounted,[1] which succeeded in driving Sheikh Ahmed over the border into Turkey by July. Later, by an agreement between Britain, Turkey and Iraq, the Sheikh and his family were allowed to return to Iraq, where they lived under surveillance, first at Nasiriya, and then at Suleimaniya.

The Barzanis did not remain quiet for long. They rose in revolt in 1934, and again in 1935, under the leadership of Khalil Khushawi, who defied a series of combined operations by both the Turks and Iraqis for several months, successfully dodging to and fro across that frontier, destroying villages, looting, killing and wreaking vengeance on those who opposed him and on his traditional enemies. By the end of 1935 most of his followers had been caught, and several of them were executed. Khalil Khushawi reappeared in Iraq in midwinter, only to be killed in an engagement in March 1936. At about the same period in the tribal areas near Suleimaniya and the Persian border another rebel leader, Said Mohammed Pichkola, was active operating and raiding from Persian territory. After being finally cornered he surrendered in August 1935, to be pardoned by the Iraqi Government.

When the British Mandate for Iraq terminated in October 1932, racial bitterness remained, much of which was against the implanted Assyrians, perhaps because they had been used so much in punitive operations by the British. The Iraqi Government took a strong line against them, and the new Iraqi Army was quick to stamp on the slightest sign of dissidence, sometimes behaving with extreme severity. On occasions the Army got out of hand. For example, in August 1933 units under the command of General Bakr Sidki massacred some 315 Assyrians at Simel, in Mosul province, near the Syrian border. There were similar incidents at Alkush and Dohuk at about the same period. Many Assyrian villages were looted and

---

[1] 'The RAF bombed Barzan, destroying 1,365 houses', according to Ghassemlou.

destroyed by the Army, and the Mar Shimun, the Assyrian religious leader, was exiled to Cyprus, from where he went to the USA.

The export of oil from Iraq, which commenced in 1934, gave promise of prosperity to the new state, but civilian government did not last long. On the 28th October 1936 there was an Iraqi Army coup led by General Bakr Sidki, who was a Kurd. He was assassinated on the 8th August 1937, but the Army remained dominant in politics, being influenced by four senior officers who became known as the Golden Square. In December 1938 Nuri Said assumed the Premiership for the fifth time. By then all seemed to be quiet in Kurdish territory; the tribal leaders had been arrested or driven over the borders, and government administration was introduced for the first time in the Pishdar region. The property and lands of Sheikh Mahmoud Barzanji, confiscated in 1931, were restored to him, while within the Iraqi Army the bickering between Arab and Kurd lessened and discipline seemed to improve.

Over the border, to the west of Iraq, the Kurds in the mountainous areas of eastern Turkey who revolted against the central Government were put down far more brutally and completely. The Kurds living in the mountains around Lake Van had always been a particular centre of revolt and source of trouble to the pre-World War I Turkish governments. The chief Kurdish town in Turkey was Diarbekr, which was officially quoted as having 63,108 inhabitants in 1939. Turkish victory over the Greeks in 1922, and the consequent emergence of Turkey as a military power, banished all thoughts of granting autonomy to the Kurds, Armenians or other minorities. The 12th of President Wilson's famous 14 Points was coldly ignored.[1] For a couple of years no attempt was made to penetrate the Kurdish mountains; indeed, Kemal Ataturk, in his bid to unify his country, used Kurdish tribesmen on several occasions to help him, but he had no place for an independent Kurdistan in his new Turkey. In October 1923 the National Assembly declared Turkey a republic and Kemal Ataturk was elected President.

To the north-east of Turkey during this period the Soviet Union[2]

[1] The 12th Point included '. . . other nationalities which are now under Turkish rule should be assured an undoubted security of life and an absolute unmolested opportunity of autonomous development'.

[2] At first it was called the Russian Soviet Federative Socialist Republic (RSFSR), which in 1923 gave way to the Union of Soviet Socialist Republics (USSR), now more familiarly known as the Soviet Union, an expression that will be used for convenience.

had ruthlessly suppressed all Kurdish attempts to express their nationalism in its territory, and Russian troops advanced as far south as Mount Ararat, technically on Turkish soil, where they laid a two-year siege to a group of rebellious Kurds, who were eventually forced to melt away into the adjacent mountains of Turkey and Persia.

The Turkish Kurds did not like Kemal Ataturk's attitude towards them, and when, in March 1924, he abolished the Caliphate, they rose in rebellion against him. Their leader was Sheikh Said, of Palu, who headed the powerful Nakshabandi tribe.[1] There had already been deep rumblings of discontent against the new Government during the previous month, but almost entirely on religious grounds. There was little of a national character about this rising, its main object being to overthrow the Government and restore the Caliphate. By mid-March the revolt was gaining ground and rapidly spreading to the east and south, but it was checked when swift, decisive action was taken by the Turkish Army which, with large numbers of troops committed to this operation,[2] systematically surrounded the rebels. The revolt ended in April 1924, when Sheikh Said and other leaders were captured. As the Army advanced, field tribunals were set up which administered hard justice on the spot, and on the 30th June Sheikh Said and 46 of his supporters were executed. After the revolt some '80,000 troops concentrated in the area, despoiling it'.[3] In all some 206 villages were destroyed, 8,758 houses were burnt and 15,200 people were killed.[4]

Kemal Ataturk declared that the revolt had been a Kurdish national one, but this was probably not quite accurate as the movement had more of a religious than a national impetus. Severe restrictions against Kurdish nationalism were put into effect, all Kurdish mosques were closed, all Kurdish associations were dissolved, Kurdish ceremonies and meetings were banned, and their traditional dress was proscribed, but the implementation of these repressive measures was largely overshadowed by Kemal Ataturk's other innovations, designed to bring Turkey into the modern world, such as banning the fez, an act which in itself caused an uproar. This totally unsympathetic attitude towards them by the Turkish Govern-

---

[1] Purists may insist that the Nakshabandi are a dervish confraternity found in various Moslem lands and should not properly be described as a tribe.
[2] '35,000 troops and 12 aircraft', according to Ghassemlou.
[3] Ghassemlou.   [4] Ghassemlou.

ment caused many Kurds to move over the borders into Persia or Iraq; the Soviet Union had firmly closed its frontiers to them.

The chastened Kurds lay low for a while, and the next Kurdish insurrection in Turkey did not occur until 1927, when Sheikh Ihsan Nuri organized a resistance movement in the areas to the north and east of Mount Ararat. This dragged on spasmodically for almost three years, during which period successive Turkish military operations were mounted against him, until he was crushed in 1930. Another Kurdish revolt in eastern Turkey had been harshly stamped out in the previous year (1929).

In 1927, Kurdish nationalist organizations merged into the Khoybun, a body that had been originally formed in World War I by Kurdish exiles, largely intellectuals, which had the object of claiming independence for regions where Kurds were in the majority. It held its first Congress in the Lebanon. At about this period (the late 1920s) it had some contact and influence with the Kurds living in Turkey and claimed that it had given considerable support to the Sheikh Ihsan Nuri revolt near Mount Ararat.

Unrest, tinged with nationalism, had begun to germinate in other parts of Kurdish territory in Turkey. In June 1930 some dissident Kurds, led by a group of ex-officers who had served in the Turkish Army, rose in revolt. The Turkish Army, strongly supported by the Air Force, moved against the rebels in strength, and with ruthless brutality defeated them within a month. After this campaign harsh punitive treatment was meted out.[1] In these latter military operations against the Kurdish rebels there had been a degree of co-operation between the Turkish and Persian Armies along their mutual frontier areas, and the Persian Government had in fact permitted a large Turkish force to use Persian territory to assault the Kurdish rebels from the rear. After this defeat the Khoybun rapidly lost influence. The Turkish Premier, Ismet Inonu, himself a Kurd, had declared while the campaign was in progress that the 'revolt, now continuing in our eastern provinces for the fifth year [was] incited by foreign intrigue and [had] already lost half its strength'.[2]

Once the 1930 Revolt had been quelled, the Kurds in the mountains were again left much to their own devices until mid-1937, when the Turkish Government began a deliberate policy of penetration, pacification and of imposing firm governmental control. As military

[1] '165 villages and 6,816 houses were destroyed', according to Ghassemlou.
[2] Ghassemlou.

forces systematically advanced into Kurdish territory, a chain of police posts was established, and this caused another Kurdish revolt, led by Seyid Reza, to erupt in June (1937) in the Dersim region. The rebels were joined by a group of Kurds from Syria, then under French control, which country had the declared intention of establishing an independent Kurdistan in eastern Turkey. The French in Syria at that time were secretly in sympathy with Kurdish national aspirations, and had given some clandestine help and support. In this revolt it was alleged by the Turkish Government, but never satisfactorily established, that arms had been supplied to the Kurdish rebels by the Soviet Union.

-The Turkish Army moved against the rebels and a four-month campaign ensued. This time, as they penetrated, Government troops remained to impose civil administration on the areas. The Kurds were gradually disarmed, steps were taken to detribalize them, further efforts were made to discourage national dress and language, and Turkish became compulsory. Kurdish titles were abolished, sheikhs were deported from their localities, and whole sections of tribes were forcibly removed to other districts. The construction of roads, for which Kurds were impressed as labourers, enabled the frontiers with Iraq and Persia to be more effectively guarded, thus reducing the incidence of arms smuggling and illegal crossing. The long tradition of Kurdish lawlessness in Turkey was made the official excuse for such harsh action, but soon the Turkish authorities were able to boast, with much truth, that they had no 'Kurdish problem'. The word itself was banned, and the Kurds became officially known as Mountain Turks who 'had forgotten their mother-tongue'. During these several military operations there had been spasms of fierce fighting between Turkish soldiers and the Kurds, in which occasionally heavy casualties were incurred. It was not possible to ascertain precise figures, as the Turkish Government discouraged publicity and refused to give any details.

To the east of Iraq, immediately after World War I, the northern parts of Persia had dissolved into chaos, the central Government at Teheran having completely lost all control; these areas had been ravaged by both Bolsheviks and units of the new Russian Red Army, and by aggressive, well-armed bodies of Kurdish tribesmen untrammelled by any authoritative curbs. In Teheran returned nationalist elements grouped together, and in 1921 a coup d'état led by Reza Khan Pahlavi, a former officer in the Cossack Force, was effected. He became the Minister of War; in 1923 he became the Premier and in 1925 he was elected Shah. Persia still had no conventional regular or conscript army; its only effective military bodies were the Cossack Force in the north and the armed gendarmerie. First of all Reza Khan laid the foundations of a national regular army and slowly built it up. He disbanded the gendarmerie, and formed other units to police the provinces, some of which were barely submissive to the central Government. The Cossack Force, in which Persian officers had replaced Russian ones, was reorganized and brought into the framework of the Army.

In 1920 Simko, Agha of the 40,000 strong Shikak tribe of Kurds, operating in the region just to the east of Lake Rezaieh, raised revolt in the name of Kurdish nationalism. Although he had some initial successes against units of the Cossack Force and the gendarmerie, he was considerably restricted in movement owing to the presence of Red Army troops, who did not leave Persia until May 1922. In July of that year elements of the Persian Army moved against him successfully, forcing Simko to escape to Turkey, where he was interned. He was pardoned by the Shah two years later and allowed to return to Persia, but in 1926 he instigated another revolt, which was crushed by the reorganized Persian Army. After this, Simko fled first to Iraq and then to Turkey. Yet another insurrection was ignited among the Persian Kurds in 1930, in which Simko took an active part. This time the Persian Army operated in conjunction with that of Turkey along their common border. In the course of one of the actions Simko was killed in an ambush.[1] These Simko revolts had practically all taken place in the Persian province of Azerbaijan.

Although they claimed to have a Kurdish national character and motive, the Persian authorities asserted that the Simko revolts were simply the actions of a tribal brigand, with ambitions only for personal power and loot. After 1930 the new Persian Army, now in a more stable condition, commenced a systematic penetration into the Kurdish mountains, when roads were constructed and police posts built. Dissident or influential sheikhs were sent to Teheran, literally as hostages, or removed from their tribal areas to live under surveillance elsewhere, while efforts were made to discourage Kurdish national dress, customs and language, and to enforce the use of the Persian tongue. Although they were allowed to retain their arms,

[1] On the 21st June 1930.

30

under the strong hand of Reza Shah the Kurds in Persia remained comparatively passive until World War II. The last revolt in this phase of Kurdish discontent in Persia occurred in 1931, and was led by Sheikh Tafar of the powerful Hamadan tribe. It was put down harshly, after which the Persian Government was able to declare that it 'had no Kurdish problem', which to a certain degree was true for a decade.

As for the degree of freedom, political and otherwise, enjoyed by the Kurds in the four countries in which they lived on the outbreak of World War II, those in the Soviet Union, estimated to be about 100,000, had to all external appearances been completely pressed into the Soviet socialistic mould, a slight trace of traditionalism but none of nationalism being permitted. The Kurds were not allowed to carry arms, and neither were any Kurdish nationalist or political organizations permitted. They mainly lived in areas around Talin and Alagor, in the Soviet Socialist Republic of Armenia. The Kurds in Syria, officially quoted as numbering about 200,000, were smiled upon by the French authorities, who regarded them as a favoured minority provided they behaved themselves, as they were a useful counter-balance to other minorities and factions within the country. They were encouraged to think in terms of an independent Kurdistan, but although Kurdish political organizations were permitted, in fact their political freedom was only partial. They were not allowed to carry arms, but generally they were left to their own devices so long as they took care not to displease their French overlords. In Persia, where there were officially about 1 million Kurds, they were being slowly disarmed, their language and customs were discouraged, and their sheikhs were taken as hostages for the tribes' good behaviour. Like the remainder of the Persians under the dictatorial Reza Shah, they had limited political freedom within an approved Persian context, but of Kurdish national aspirations they were allowed none at all. In the mountains they were kept under firm control by the close presence of the Army and the Air Force. The Persian Government refused to admit the existence of any 'Kurdish problem' whatever. In Turkey, a country that did not admit to the existence of any Kurds, let alone a 'Kurdish problem', there were about 3 million 'Mountain Turks', who were under strict governmental control; the least indication of any dissidence meant the removal, and possible detention of sheikhs and their families, or even whole tribes. They had been largely disarmed, their language and dress were discouraged and a programme of detribalization was being forced through. It was in Iraq, where there were officially 1·2 million Kurds, that they had the greatest freedoms, as most of the tribal Kurds retained their arms, customs and language, and were able to indulge in political activities provided they did not demand outright autonomy or independence.

The sum of these official figures indicates there were only about 5·5 million Kurds in these four countries. The Kurds themselves, however, insisted that the figures were deliberately minimized for political reasons, and that the true total should be nearer 8 million, as there were at least 4 million Kurds in Turkey, 2 million in Persia, 1·5 million in Iraq, and at least 400,000 in Syria.

A few brief facts and comments on the Kurds, their way of life and characteristics, are necessary to form a backcloth against which to unfold the story of their subsequent fortunes. In 1939 the area in which the Kurds formed the majority probably comprised some 250,000 square miles, the core of which was a land mass of mountainous terrain. Some authorities give a considerably lower assessment than this, but there were few precise ethnic boundaries, and in the fringe areas Kurds tended to be interspersed, or even intermixed, with other races. The Kurdish tribes inhabited a rough, half-moon-shaped 'blob', some 700 miles from end to end, extending from eastern Turkey to Kermanshah province in Persia, its inner arc including the north-east tip of Syria and large sectors of Iraq as far south as the old Turkish vilayet of Mosul, while its outer arc encompassed a sliver of Soviet soil and Lake Rezaieh in Persia. Areas in which Kurds are in the majority will be referred to as 'Kurdish territory' to avoid any national or political connotation.

The Kurds have their own language which, as both Kurds and Persians come from the same stock, can be conveniently described as somewhat akin to Persian. There are three main dialects, Zaza, Gurani and Kermanji, of which there are local variants. Zaza is spoken in the northern parts of Turkey and the Persian province of Azerbaijan, while Gurani is spoken mainly in the Persian province of Kermanshah; neither is written. Kermanji is the most important dialect, being used by over 50 per cent of the Kurds throughout the remainder of Kurdish territory, especially in Iraq. It has been reduced to writing, it is the semi-official Kurdish language, and it was taught, for example, in schools in Kurdish territory in Iraq under the British Mandate.

The Kurds are all of the Moslem faith.[1] There are two main sects, the Shias and the Sunnis; doctrinal and other differences distinguish them. The Kurds living in Iraq, in the Persian province of Kurdistan, in the western part of Persian Azerbaijan, and some two-thirds of those in Turkey are Sunnis, while the remainder are Shias. A few tiny extremist sects also exist, such as the Ali-Ilahis, in the Persian province of Kermanshah, who believe Ali, son-in-law of the Prophet and the fourth Caliph, to be an emanation of God. Animosity between Sunni Kurds and Shia Kurds in Persian Azerbaijan occurred from time to time on religious issues, but otherwise in Kurdish territory there was generally little active friction between the two sects.

A mere century or so previously the Kurds had been a pastoral and somewhat nomadic race, a loose collection of shifting tribes, or groups of tribes; units varied from fewer than 500 families to over 3,000. Smaller tribes, for protection and self-preservation, had to ally themselves to larger ones, or with each other, and so federations formed and crumbled as loyalties and circumstances changed. Right up until the end of the 19th century the sight of a large tribal federation, with all its livestock, moving across the mountains and plains of the northern parts of the Middle East in search of fresh grazing, was both splendid and ominous—as nomadic Kurds moved like a plague of locusts, feeding and feuding.

In the mid-19th century about one-third of the Kurds were nomadic, and indeed until World War I national frontiers were of no significance to them. The final demarcation and closing of international frontiers after that war put a stop to the long traditional summer and winter migrations of the Kurds, which in itself hit some tribes hard economically and so made for additional discontent. In some instances artificial barriers formed as these frontiers cut arbitrarily through the territory of certain tribes, splitting them asunder. For example, the territory of the numerous and powerful Herki tribe now lay part in Turkey, part in Iraq and part in Persia, while the Shikak tribe was partly in Turkey and partly in Persia.

Tobacco cultivation began to change this nomadic way of life. As it was a quick and profitable crop with a ready market, several tribes settled down to grow it. Soon some tribes were nomadic for just part of the year. As tobacco and other forms of cultivation were adopted

[1] In Iraq there were about 50,000 Yazidis, or 'Peacock' (or 'Devil') Worshippers, a religious sect within the Kurdish people.

the nomadic and semi-nomadic tribes found it increasingly difficult both to get to, and to use, good grazing grounds which had become 'settled', and consequently many inter-tribal quarrels and fights were over such issues. For example, the Herki tribe, one of the largest, with an estimated 30,000 members, was semi-nomadic and claimed dominance over an area in Persia to the west and south of Lake Rezaieh. Consequently it was the main enemy of adjacent settled tribes, such as the Barzanis (in Iraq), which blocked off its traditional grazing routes. The settled tribes usually had barely enough grazing for their own animals all the year round, let alone hundreds or thousands of others.

The Kurdish tribes were subdivided into clans and groups of families, each being always on the defensive, ever suspicious of the others, and intent on survival. In Persia there were estimated to be some 60 tribes, of which probably about 15 could be classed as major ones, the largest being the Kalhor, settled to the west of Kermanshah, which had some 120,000 members. In Iraq there were some 22 major and 54 minor ones, while in Syria there were about 12 tribes. In the Soviet Union the tribal structure in Kurdish territory as such was reported to have been almost completely nullified, while in Turkey, although the old traditional tribal organization was known still to exist, no precise details of the individual tribes, or their numbers and locations, were available because of official policy. Old reports and estimates were either out of date or unreliable. Each man owed complete allegiance to his family and tribe. The sheikh, who was both head of the tribe and a local religious leader, settled all disputes within it according to tribal law and customs. Under tribal law, for example, murders could be cancelled out by blood money or marriage, while men could be executed for theft. Within the tribe there was a fairly strict moral code of behaviour in their dealings with each other, but this seems not always to have obtained in the case of inter-tribal matters, which were frequently marred by bad faith and treachery. Lacking national cohesion, tribes at times allied themselves to enemies of other Kurdish tribes and fought against them for an alien foe.

Most of the tribesmen were clustered in small mountain villages. The local sheikh lived in a fairly solid stone house, built for defence. His followers occupied hovels constructed of stone, wood and mud. In the mountains the Kurds existed sparsely, mainly on pastoral and agricultural produce such as milk, cheese, eggs, fruit and potatoes;

few ate meat, either chicken or goat, more than once a week. Wheat, barley and maize were grown, which when ground and made into a flattish loaf of bread formed the basis of their daily diet. The more prosperous, and those settled on richer agricultural land, naturally fared better. The prestige drink for all who could afford it was tea with sugar, which was offered to guests.

Kurdish dress was perhaps the only feature, apart from language, that tended to distinguish them as a race. It consisted of baggy trousers secured at the ankle (although Barzan trousers, were 'flared' at the bottoms), a cummerbund or heavy leather belt, shirt, longish jacket frequently embroidered in colour, and a turban, the colour, fringe or mode of wearing often denoting the individual tribe. The men invariably wore the 'khanjar', a curved dagger, in the belt as a symbol of manhood and warrior status. Much favoured were bandoliers with cartridges exposed, crossed over the chest, and a weapon, even an ancient firearm, was carried as a prized prestige accessory. Frequently worn were items of cast-off Western clothing, such as jackets, shirts, coats and raincoats. In extremely cold weather the Kurds simply put on more coats, eventually being almost smothered under layers of clothing. A few modern-minded sheikhs, educated Kurds and young revolutionaries liked to wear Western-type lounge suits and trilby hats. Kurdish women were not veiled and wore traditional dress of their own.

Like most mountain races, the Kurds tended to have better physique and to be slightly taller than some of the surrounding races, such as the lowland Arabs, whom they terrorized for years. Many Kurds had light skins and blue eyes, perhaps a heritage from invaders of centuries before. Medical facilities in Kurdish territory were almost non-existent, and health was a problem, especially in severe winters. In particular they were plagued with cholera, owing to the often insanitary conditions and the foulness of village wells. There was a continuous exodus of young men from the tribes into the towns to find work. The majority did not return, and produced a growing element of detribalized urban Kurds. Many Kurds served in the armed forces of the states they resided in, while in Persia and Iraq they also entered government service and the professions, as well as practically all trades and jobs, especially in the expanding oilfields. In both Iraq and Persia, Kurds had held office in governments, and been involved in national politics for some years, being represented more than in strict proportion to their overall numbers. In the 1920s a Kurdish intelligentsia began to appear, a product of improved educational opportunities.

Since ancient times the Kurds have been renowned for their martial virtues; indeed, from the days when the Romans eagerly sought to enlist them as auxiliaries they have regarded the profession of arms highly and appreciated feats of valour and martial qualities. It has been said that the form of Kurdish family and tribal life is based not only on a social but on a military pattern as a response over the centuries to circumstances that have compelled them to be always on their guard and ready to fight at a moment's notice. At the beginning of the 20th century, instead of paying taxes, some tribes sent members to be soldiers, especially in areas under Turkish control. Periodically, when in search of plunder, the Kurds, mounted on small, sturdy ponies and armed with sword and lance, emerged from their mountains to sweep down on to the plains below; their fierce cavalry charges and wild war cries gained them a formidable reputation. In the late 19th century, when the Kurds began to obtain modern rifles, their traditional form of warfare suddenly changed, and their cavalry shock tactics gave way to dismounted 'fire-and-movement' infiltration methods, but in the outside world their old cavalry reputation lingered on. Horses were still used by Kurdish warriors, but mainly to carry them into battle, when they dismounted to fight. They no longer charged in mass, although sometimes they did so to cross open spaces, to frighten the enemy, or to get closer to him quickly. The rifle was now the Kurds' primary weapon. Swords and lances were hardly ever used in battle, as in any hand-to-hand fighting the dagger was preferred. Sometimes the Kurds would fire their rifles from horseback without taking aim to try to demoralize the enemy, or horsemen would carry another man quickly forward to a better tactical position, and then gallop back out of rifle range. Generally the horse was only used for warlike purposes and seldom purely for travel, because it was often quicker to go on foot, as the rider invariably had to dismount to lead the animal both up and down the steeper mountain slopes. The beast of burden in Kurdish territory was the humble donkey. The Kurdish method of attacking a village was first of all to occupy the surrounding hills and then creep closer, using 'fire-and-movement' as necessary. In defence of a village the women would join in the fighting and give a good account of themselves.

In the past Kurdish wars had usually been for plunder, to dominate good grazing grounds, or when bribed to fight by someone else. Whenever losses became heavy they stopped fighting, divided any loot and returned home again. They were able to do this because generally they were left completely alone in their mountains, where the terrain presented too many hazards to an attacker and their war-like reputation was a deterrent. It was not until the pacification campaigns of the 1920s that the Kurds were faced for the first time by systematic attempts by trained troops to penetrate and remain in the heart of their homeland and bring them to heel. However, the Kurds quickly mastered the art of defensive mountain warfare, becoming adept at ambushes, sniping and picqueting heights; in these types of operations they had several successes in cutting off and ambushing Government forces, which were often saved only by direct aircraft intervention. But, as will be seen, Government troops developed the practice of building 'sangars', rough stone defensive shelters, as they moved forward, into which they were able to retire hastily if fired upon. This brought about a sort of stalemate, as the Kurds did not develop a counter to put into effect before they were invariably scattered by aerial bombing.

2

RISE OF KURDISH NATIONALISM

'The Turks will never obey the Kurds, nor the Kurds the
Turks.'

Baha al-Deen (Biographer of Saladin)

During hostilities between the Axis Powers and the Allies during
World War II, and in the concurrent and subsequent power struggle
between the Western Powers and the Soviet Union in the Middle
East, Kurdish nationalism was kindled. It flourished to culminate in
the establishment of a small Kurdish republic, which was quickly
extinguished when Soviet occupation troops withdrew from
Persia.

In the months prior to World War II serious Nazi German attempts had been made to penetrate and influence Iraq, especially the
Army and the Futuwa (the Iraqi Youth Movement), which had some
success, so much so that when the war broke out in September 1939
the Iraqi Government only severed diplomatic relations with Germany—a minimum requirement in accordance with the Anglo-Iraqi
Treaty—but did not declare war, or even mobilize its Army, which
then had a standing strength of about 32,000. Of the planned four
divisions, only two had materialized. Anti-British sentiment had
arisen in Iraq in protest against the British Zionist policy in Palestine,
and when in October 1939 the ex-Mufti of Jerusalem arrived in
Baghdad he was able to fan this.

After the fall of France in 1940 and under the impact of the initial
German victories, British stock fell to a very low ebb in the Middle
East, and sympathy for Germany rose correspondingly. When Italy
entered the war in June (1940) it seemed as though the Axis Powers
were the dominant ones, and there was talk—particularly loud in
military circles—of completely breaking away from British influence.
The Italian Embassy in Baghdad became a centre for anti-Allied
espionage. On the 1st April 1941 there was an army coup, led by the
Golden Square, which made Rashid Ali Gailani, who had strong
anti-British views, the Premier. A German military mission arrived

in Baghdad, King Feisal II[1] was placed under house arrest, and Prince Abdul Illah, the Regent, fled the capital, as did Nuri Said and other personalities.

The Anglo-Iraqi Treaty of 1930 provided, among other things, that Britain could maintain air bases at Habbaniya and Basra, have the right to transport troops and military supplies across Iraq, and in time of war have the use of existing communications. On the 18th April 1941 British troops disembarked at Basra, but a request to land more was turned down by Rashid Ali. Despite this another brigade arrived at the same port on the 28th, which provoked Iraqi action. Hoping for German ground and air support, Rashid Ali became bolder, and ordered an Iraqi force, eventually numbering over 10,000, to move against the British air base at Habbaniya, but it ran into unexpectedly prickly opposition. German air support did not materialize in time and after four days of fighting around the air base, that ended on the 6th May, the Iraqi units were forced to withdraw. By the 30th May, after further actions, British troops entered Baghdad, and a pro-British Government was installed. Rashid Ali, the ex-Mufti of Jerusalem, and others had fled, while the Regent, Prince Abdul Illah, returned. The following month there was a brief, four-day campaign (8th–12th June) against Vichy French forces in Syria, which resulted in an armistice satisfactory to the Allies.

Although Persia[2] had declared its neutrality in 1939, the large German mission operating in Teheran caused British anxiety. In June 1941, when the Soviet Union entered the war, Persia again declared its neutrality, but this brought about a changed situation. Persian territory now formed a much-needed land corridor along which the Allies wanted to send military supplies to the Soviet Union from the Persian Gulf. Also, Persia had vital oil. Early in August the Persian Government turned down a request from Britain to expel all German nationals from its soil, and a subsequent joint British-Soviet note, conveying a similar demand, also received an unsatisfactory reply. German prestige remained high in Persia, the Shah tended to be anti-Russian in his views, and there remained an underlying fear of Russian intentions. The two-pronged British-Soviet invasion of Persia began on the 25th August 1941, when British troops landed at dawn

[1] King Ghazi, who had succeeded his father, Feisal I, in 1933, died in a car accident in April 1939, and was succeeded by his infant son, Feisal II.

[2] Persia officially became Iran (the old traditional name for the country) in 1935: in 1957 the Government allowed the name Persia to be used again. For clarity in this narrative it will be called Persia throughout.

to seize the oil refinery at Abadan. They then moved on to take possession of other oilfields and strategic points, while Soviet troops advanced southwards.

The Persian Army, with a strength of about 127,000 men, a few tanks and some mountain artillery (its Air Force had about twenty obsolete aircraft), was hardly able to put up any serious resistance at all. On the 28th it was ordered to cease fire by the Shah, who abdicated in favour of his son, Mohammed Raza Pahlavi. There was a two-week pause in Allied advances, after which, as the terms of the armistice did not seem to be implemented, on the 17th September Teheran was jointly occupied by British and Soviet troops for a month, while a government favourable to the Allies was installed. The British occupied key points in Persia south of a rough line through Sardasht, Saqqiz and Zanjan, while the Russians did likewise to the north of it. This dual occupation lasted until after the end of World War II, during which period some 5 million tons of supplies passed along this route from the Persian Gulf to Russia. A Tripartite Treaty between Britain, the Soviet Union and Persia provided for this joint Allied occupation to terminate six months after the end of the war. Although the new Shah remained in Teheran, a large number of prominent personalities left the capital and took no part in the wartime government of their country.

During this joint Allied invasion of Persia many Persian Army units simply disintegrated, and the Kurds were able to acquire a number of arms and quantities of small arms ammunition. The Allied Powers generally left the Persian Government to enforce its writ on the civil side as best it could, and in the absence of a strong central authority the Kurds quickly became a law unto themselves. The several Kurdish sheikhs who had been in enforced residence in Teheran were allowed to return to their tribes, and they had an unsettling effect on them. At one stage, for example, in May 1942, such was the extent of lawlessness that the Soviet authorities allowed Persian Army units to move into the Soviet-occupied province of Azerbaijan to take punitive action against Kurdish insurgents in the area of Lake Rezaieh, although they normally insisted that Persian troops should stay south of the Sardasht-Zanjan line.

Soon the Soviet Union was hard at work in a subtle manner to subvert both the Kurds and the Azerbaijanis in northern Persia, the ultimate object being to form them into semi-autonomous, Communist-orientated groups that would either opt for incorporation into the Soviet Union after the war, or at least be strongly pro-Soviet in character. Sovietized Azerbaijanis infiltrated nationalistic and political organizations or founded new ones. There were about 2·5 million Azerbaijanis in Soviet Azerbaijan, and some 4 million to the south of them in the Persian province of Azerbaijan, all of whom were traditionally hostile to the Kurds.

In Kurdish territory Soviet political subversion made slower progress, perhaps because of the traditional hostility of Moslem tribes towards Russia, although Soviet political agents were busy. Shortly after the Soviet Union entered the war, a group of prominent Kurdish sheikhs and politicians were invited to Baku, in Russia, but this visit was not a complete success; it was not until the 16th September 1942 that a Kurdish organization consisting of small secret cells—on the usual Communist pattern—known as the 'Komula', was formed, under Soviet sponsorship, in the remote town of Mahabad, just south of Lake Rezaieh. Its full title was 'Komula i Zhian I Kurdistan', which was usually translated as the 'Committee of the Life of Kurdistan', and occasionally as the 'Youth of Kurdistan', but was most commonly referred to as the Komula, or Committee. There was no Soviet military presence in Mahabad, then a town of some 16,000 people, and Persian authority was only nominal. In May 1943 a group of Kurds attacked the police station, killing several Persian policemen, after which all direct Persian authority was removed. In April 1943 a Central Committee was formed and the underground activities of the Komula, under Soviet instigation, spread throughout the territory under Soviet occupation and seeped southwards until checked by the presence of Persian military units.

The older Kurdish political organization, the Khoybun, flickered into life again, but in general it was out of touch with the tribal sheikhs in the mountains, and had only limited influence in the towns of Iraq, where it tended to be overshadowed by another Kurdish political organization, the Heva. The Heva, or Hewa (the Kurdish word for 'hope'), was the other main Kurdish political organization; there had been and were others, or traces of others existed, but they did not amount to much as political instruments. It was a predominantly Iraqi organization that developed into what was virtually the Kurdish Nationalist Party. Founded in Kirkuk in late 1942, it developed strong branches in the main towns in Iraq, such as Baghdad, Mosul, Suleimaniya and Arbil, but it also had a number of Persian and Turkish Kurds as members. The Heva contained the Kurdish

41

intelligentsia, such as it was, and many government officials and army officers, its object being Kurdish autonomy within the state of Iraq, but it had a strong left-wing bias. Soon after its formation it moved its headquarters to Baghdad and issued a newspaper, *Azdai* (Freedom), which expounded a socialist doctrine and published Communist propaganda. At this stage the Heva did not appreciate that its views were so contrary to those held by the tribal sheikhs—the grass roots of Kurdish power—and for that reason alone it never really gained paramount influence.

National Communist parties had been banned in some Middle East countries before World War II, but they mostly managed to exist underground. The Iraqi Communist Party was formed in 1934, and had always been illegal, small and unpopular; a drive had been made against it in 1938 by the Government. The Iraqi Communists had supported Rashid Ali and adopted an anti-British line, which made for British occupational difficulties in 1942, but when the Soviet Union entered the war their attitude swung sharply the other way and they gave massive support to the Allies. The Communists were not united. There were two main underground groups, the League of Iraqi Communists, which contained many idealists and intelligentsia, and the ICP proper, which had a much more practical outlook. The ICP issued a secret news-sheet, *Al-Qaida*, and gained a following in Kurdish territory among the younger, educated Kurds. In 1944 Nuri Said, once again the Premier, refused permission for the two groups to merge and openly form a People's Party. However, in due course Nuri Said had reluctantly to come to terms with the Soviet Union, which he deeply mistrusted, and in November 1944 a Soviet Ambassador was appointed to Baghdad, after which the Iraqi Communists operated almost openly, recruiting and gathering strength, as they calculated that the Soviet Union would not allow Nuri Said to crack down on them too heavily.

In Persia, when the old Shah abdicated in September 1941, political parties were once again permitted to operate, and a few were resurrected or formed, but none amounted to much except the Tudeh, which was almost Communist in outlook and practice. The Tudeh, strongly supported by the Soviet Union and courted by Britain, which saw it as the most stable force in the rickety Persian political structure, quickly gained prominence and published a newspaper, *Azhir*.

The Kurds maintained their suspicious attitude towards other races and countries, and accordingly Soviet agents had no easy task. Nor did the Iraqi Government, although invariably throughout the war it contained one or more Kurds. For their part the Arabs still mistrusted the Kurds, and recalled that in the battle for the British air base at Habbaniya, in 1941, the British had taken arms from Arab members of the Iraq Levies and given them to Kurds and Assyrians who, it was alleged and widely believed, used them to kill many Arabs living near the camp area. While the Arab parts of Iraq were fertile ground for Axis agents (a situation that did not basically change until after the Battle of Stalingrad), the Kurds were far less susceptible to Axis attempts to subvert them. The last such attempt occurred in November 1944, when four German agents, all Iraqis, were dropped from a German plane near Mosul. Two of them were quickly captured, while the other two escaped.

In many parts of Kurdish territory in Persia self-appointed sheikhs rose to dominate small areas, valleys or towns; often the central Government in Teheran had no option but to confirm their appointments. After some reorganization the Persian Army, this time with some Soviet approbation, re-entered several of the towns it had previously evacuated and regained control for the Persian Government, the notable exception being Mahabad. One old Kurdish rebel, Sheikh Hama Rashid, had taken over the town and district of Saqqiz, and remained 'independent' until army units drove him out into Iraq in 1942, where he was arrested. During this period there were requests from sheikhs for sectors of Kurdish territory to be incorporated into the British occupation zone, both in Iraq and Persia, but these were refused.

Now comes more fully into the story one of the, if not the, most colourful and important of all Kurdish nationalist leaders, Mullah Mustafa Barzani,[1] who had been living under house arrest at Suleimaniya since the failure of the Barzani-inspired insurrection of 1932, which had been led by his elder brother, Sheikh Ahmed Barzani. In June 1943 Mullah Mustafa escaped from Suleimaniya, crossed into Persia and made his way back into Iraq to reach his home town, Barzan. There he preached Kurdish nationalism in a vague sort of way, gaining widespread support against the unpopular Iraqi Government, which the Kurds considered to be anti-Kurdish.

Just over the border in Turkey, in July 1943, another Kurdish sheikh, Said Biroki, raised some tribes in revolt against the Turkish

[1] In this instance Mullah is a forename and not a religious title.

43

Government, attacking police and frontier posts and demanding autonomy. In conjunction with Sheikh Said Biroki, Mullah Mustafa took the field with his armed followers, and also raided police and frontier posts in Iraq. Within a fortnight Turkish troops had captured Sheikh Said Biroki and dispersed his followers, but despite the failure of the Kurdish revolt in Turkey Mullah Mustafa continued his insurrection tactics. In October 1943 the Iraqi Government sent a small military column against him, which he trapped and defeated, and British Indian troops had to be rushed to occupy temporarily the small town of Diyana to help stabilize the situation. Mullah Mustafa's family, still under surveillance, was moved south from Suleimaniya to Hillal. His elder brother, Sheikh Ahmed, urged him to surrender, but Mullah Mustafa's successful attack on the Iraqi military column made him confident and gave him local prestige, which in turn attracted many Kurds to his banner; a few even deserted from the Iraqi Army to join him. By the end of the year Mullah Mustafa had a force of armed Kurds several hundreds strong—far too large a force for the Iraqi Army to dislodge and defeat—so Britain asked Mullah Mustafa to stop his insurgent tactics and negotiate, which he agreed to do. Throughout this revolt Mullah Mustafa had maintained a voluminous correspondence with several senior Kurdish military officers and government officials, with the British Embassy in Baghdad, and with the Iraqi Government, as well as frequently sending out emissaries to neighbouring tribes to enlist their support. The Iraqi Government offered Mullah Mustafa the alternative of crossing into Persia or of living with the Pishdar tribe, north-east of Suleimaniya. He rejected the offer and maintained his demands for Kurdish rights. Proposals were put forward by Kurdish political organizations. Nuri Said, the Premier, under British persuasion, at first tended to be sympathetic towards them, but as Kurdish demands increased his Arab ministers became reluctant even to consider them. Considerable differences of view, ranging from rank feudalism to extreme socialism, existed between the Kurdish intellectuals, the detribalized Kurds working in non-Kurdish territory and towns, such as Kirkuk, and the tribal sheikhs. There was anti-Kurdish feeling in government circles owing to the demand for autonomy, which could only weaken Iraq as a state and could lead to separation, and also in the predominantly Arab Iraqi Army.

In January 1944 Majid Mustafa, a Kurdish Minister in Nuri Said's Government, toured Kurdish territory, removed some unpopular officials, distributed grain, appointed a Kurdish general to be Governor of Suleimaniya, and made other minor concessions. But as promises were not implemented, the Kurds became restless again, so much so that in May 1944 Nuri Said himself visited Kurdish territory and met Kurdish leaders—but not Mullah Mustafa. Sheikh Ahmed was allowed to return to live at Barzan, more minor concessions were made and more promises given. Sheikh Ahmed resumed the spiritual leadership of the Barzanis, while Mullah Mustafa retained the military and political leadership. Mullah Mustafa was intelligent, quick-witted and confident, a natural Kurdish tribal leader, but his education had been neglected and he tended to have a deep respect for learning, so he was content to accept Sheikh Ahmed's position, despite the Sheikh's occasional deviations from Moslem orthodoxy.

However, Nuri Said's Government fell, to be succeeded by one with scant sympathy for Kurdish demands. None of Nuri Said's promises was honoured, which caused deep Kurdish resentment. Alarmed by this, and by the fact that the Barzanis had become temporarily allied to their traditional enemies, the adjacent Zibaris, in July 1944 a minister from Baghdad met Kurdish leaders at Suleimaniya. More concessions were then promised, but as soon as he had left Mullah Mustafa and his followers indulged in a spate of looting Government stores and police stations.

Kurdish nationalism developed wildly in 1944. In May the Komula, in Persia, produced a Kurdish national flag, a tricolour with horizontal red, white and green bands (in fact, the Persian flag upside down). The symbol adopted was a sun, flanked by ears of wheat, with a mountain and a pen in the background. In August representatives from the main Kurdish nationalist parties from Turkey, Iraq and Persia met near Mount Dalanpur (in Iraq), near where the three countries touched, and they agreed to work for a Greater Kurdistan. A map of sorts was produced showing the areas claimed; it was exaggerated and inaccurate, as it included such towns as Kirkuk, which had as many Turks as Kurds. It also showed a Kurdish Corridor to the Mediterranean near Aleppo, in Syria.

During 1944, and well on into 1945, differences and even friction began to appear between the various Kurdish groups. For example, the Komula, whose membership had swelled to include many tribal sheikhs and personalities in the Soviet-controlled zone of Persia, sent its representatives to make contact with the Heva in Iraq, but as neither wished to be dominated by the other co-operation was limited. In Mahabad the dominant political and religious leader was Qazi Mohammed, and in October 1944 he was persuaded to join the Komula, which had its headquarters in that town. Qazi Mohammed was a lively character and a political schemer, although he has since been made out to have been a comparatively harmless leader who unfortunately became caught up in events. Qazi Mohammed did not join the Central Committee but somehow, while remaining a back-room boy, he managed to dominate the Komula, becoming its spokesman and de facto leader. From this moment onwards the Komula began to lose much of its secret character, and started openly to discuss Kurdish nationalism and aspirations.

In Iraq the Heva and the Communist factions eyed each other warily. The Communists were divided. One group, which can be called the Kurdish Communist Party because it sponsored the Kurdish cause (although it contained many non-Kurds), refused to acknowledge the authority of the Iraqi Communist Party. Relations between the Iraqi Communist groups and the Komula were cold and unco-operative, but despite these differences a loose coalition of the main Kurdish organizations came into being. It was known as the Razgar i Kurd, meaning Kurdish Deliverance, which by April 1944 had been joined by the Komula. While this Kurdish coalition seemed to be a nebulous organization, it did succeed in maintaining liaison between the several diverse groups working towards the same end, although individually they were jostling for power. Several wartime meetings, some international, resulted in vague agreements and promises of action and co-operation, but little of a substantive nature emerged.

These Kurdish political organizations, especially the Heva, continually sent letters and demands, putting their cases forward, to Allied representatives and their own governments. Mostly each acted completely independently of the others. These overtures met with little response. The Allies and the government concerned realized that the organizations had no teeth, and that the only significant military force was that led by Mullah Mustafa. It was noteworthy that Mullah Mustafa was not a member of any Kurdish political organization, although he was in touch with them all and he actively used the Heva for his own purposes. Mullah Mustafa also dispatched a stream of communications to Allied and national government representatives. In January 1945 he sent delegations to both the British Ambassador in Baghdad and the Iraqi Government, asking for Kurdish autonomy. The Heva hoped to bring Mullah Mustafa and his armed followers into their organization, which would then have made it the most formidable in Iraq, but Mullah Mustafa was not to be drawn—he had other ideas. The Heva wanted to move into the mountains and set up its headquarters at Barzan to be alongside Mullah Mustafa and his developing army, but he would not permit this and took active steps to prevent it happening by blocking the routes into the mountains. He desired the Heva to remain in Baghdad so as to be able to keep direct contact with the various Allied and government representatives, and to be his window on to the world. Positioned in Baghdad, the Heva could obtain supplies and information for him, which it could not do if buried in the remote mountains. The Heva leadership was no doubt impressed and influenced by the Yugoslav partisans who were attracting such world attention and praise, and wished to emulate them.

In March 1945 the Heva and other Kurdish organizations sent a petition to the American Ambassador in Baghdad, asking for American help to establish an independent Kurdistan, and reminding him of President Wilson's 12th Point. They all wanted to minimize Mullah Mustafa's importance; in fact, the Heva only gave him supplies and information as it wanted to use him for its own political ends, after which the intention was to abandon him. For long Mullah Mustafa had been suspicious of the Heva's intentions and it of his. There was both some friction and some co-operation between them.

However, Mullah Mustafa was already undermining his false political friends' position. In February 1945 he had formed his own party, the Freedom Party, which consisted of many Army officers, Government officials and some professional men, the majority recruited on a non-tribal basis. In an announcement on the 12th February 1945 he declared that the object of his new party was to bring about co-operation first between the tribes in the Barzan region and then between all the Kurdish tribes. He continued to recruit for his armed force and to maintain contact with the other Kurdish political organizations, while his new Freedom Party issued a stream of Kurdish nationalist propaganda. In March 1945 Nuri Said gave an amnesty to Mullah Mustafa and other Kurds who had been involved in operations against the Iraqi Army prior to February 1944.

In April 1945 a squabble at a police post near Margasur, near Barzan, led to an attack on the post and its seizure by Barzanis. This small incident sparked off others until the whole Barzani region was in a state of simmering revolt, a condition that continued throughout the summer. On the 10th August there was a major scuffle when Iraqi police tried to disarm some Barzanis, and in return the Barzanis assaulted and occupied several police posts, which caused active rebellion to break out. To quell it the Iraqi Government dispatched military columns into the mountains. The first advanced from Amadiya, while the second—of brigade strength—moved on the 25th eastwards into the Baradosti tribal area, to the west of the Barzanis. The Kurds counter-attacked, hitting the column in the flank, and they claimed to have inflicted many casualties. Another column, of about the same strength, penetrated a short way into the Zibari tribal area, just to the south of the Barzanis. Moving from Akra, it ran into an ambush organized by Mullah Mustafa himself. For two days there was critical fighting, and it was only thanks to aircraft of the RAF and the Iraqi Air Force that government troops were able to hold their positions. Aircraft also bombed Barzani villages and houses, and the Turks assisted by closing their frontier.

Realizing it was stalemate, the Iraqi Government enlisted the help of tribes traditionally hostile to the Barzanis, and thus enabled Government forces to advance again. During September Mullah Mustafa and his armed followers were gradually compressed, both from the east and south, up against the firmly barred Turkish border; then, as they felt pressure from the west as well, Mullah Mustafa realized that he was in a trap and decided to break out before it was too late. Accordingly, on the night of the 25th September, with his followers and their families, he moved to a position just to the north of Barzan from where, in the last days of the month and the first days of October, they slipped through the Iraqi Army net across the border into Persia, into Kurdish territory, to make their way towards Mahabad, then free of both Soviet and Persian military units. It was estimated that some 9,000 people, Barzanis and their allies, including families, followed Mullah Mustafa on this retreat. Of this number only about 3,000 were armed men, of whom only some 1,200[1] were personally accountable to Mullah Mustafa himself. This revolt and brief struggle against the Iraqi Government by Mullah Mustafa was notable in that it was the first time that Kurdish political organizations had actively attempted to co-operate with tribesmen in the field. Mullah Mustafa had failed to hold out, not so much because of the operations by the RAF and the Iraqi Army but because

[1] Longrigg states about 2,000—but reliable figures are scarce.

the Barzanis were so much disliked by other tribes, which could not forget their old enmity and which tended, when bribed with money or arms, to co-operate with Government forces and to forget all about the shining ideals of Kurdish nationalism. In short, Mullah Mustafa's defeat was due to the Zibaris, Baradostis and Surchis—in other words to Kurds.

The war in Europe over, the Soviet Union was anxious to make gains in northern Persia, and during the summer decided to use the Komula and Qazi Mohammed, its vociferous mouthpiece and backroom boy, as instruments for subverting Kurdish territory in Persia. In September 1945 a second party of influential Kurds, led by Qazi Mohammed, visited Baku, in the Soviet Union, for discussions. The Russians wanted the Kurds to develop a strong political framework so as to be able to exploit autonomy, and they promised financial support and arms. A printing press was sent to enable the Komula to churn out propaganda, and places were found for a few young Kurds at the Baku Military College. It was the Soviet idea that an autonomous Kurdistan would merge into an autonomous Azerbaijan, which the Russians also wanted to develop, and so form a major bloc, but Qazi Mohammed and the Kurds wanted independence. However, the Russians must have felt that they would be able to persuade the Kurds to change their minds later on, as they continued to encourage them to become independent of the Persian Government.

In October 1945, in Persian Azerbaijan, the Soviet occupation forces were slightly increased in number to provide support for the partisans, who had been armed with Soviet weapons and who had become active against such remnants of Persian authority as remained. In November bands of Azerbaijanis began taking over police posts and pushing out military detachments, which caused the withdrawal of Persian troops from Tabriz. The small brigade sent to restore Persian authority was stopped at Qazvin and prevented from entering Soviet-occupied territory. On the 12th December 1945 the Democratic Party of Azerbaijan was founded, with the aim of working for autonomy within Persia, and on the 10th January 1946 a National Government of Azerbaijan declared its independence.

Meanwhile, Mullah Mustafa, who with some 9,000 followers had arrived near Mahabad, was suspected of being a British agent, and he was treated with caution. He met Qazi Mohammed, the acknowledged leader in the town, and they agreed that the bulk of the Barzanis and their allies could stay in areas just to the north-west of

Mahabad, that is, adjacent to the Iraqi frontier, and that a number could actually live in Mahabad itself. Mullah Mustafa, with his entourage and their families, moved into Mahabad, setting up his headquarters in a hotel and taking over several houses. In view of the Barzani strength, Qazi Mohammed could hardly do anything else.

In November 1945 Qazi Mohammed had announced that the Komula, which so far had operated underground, was to come out into the open and be known as the Democratic Party of Kurdistan, the DPK.[1] With his authoritative personality he continued to dominate the new DPK as he had done the Komula, even though he did not become a member of its Central Committee or indeed hold any official position. The DPK had nationalist aims; a manifesto was issued demanding the use of the Kurdish language, self-government in local affairs, all officials to be Kurdish, the spending in Kurdish regions of all revenue collected, and the formation of a provisional council of Kurdistan. It will be seen that the DPK's initial aims were still those of autonomy and not complete independence. Under Soviet urging the DPK made an attempt to liaise with the Democratic Party of Azerbaijan, but from the start there was friction, which the Russians were unable to overcome. Mullah Mustafa retained the leadership of his own Freedom Party, and would not join the DPK; he believed in keeping his options and lines of communication open and uncommitted.

The momentum generated by the Kurds pushed them into the more ambitious project of complete independence, rather than simply that of autonomy. The promised Soviet printing press arrived in November, and Kurdish nationalist propaganda was produced in addition to a Kurdish newspaper, *Kurdistan*, which openly advocated independence. When a secret consignment of Soviet arms (believed to be about 1,200 rifles and pistols) was given to the DPK near Mahabad, the intoxication of the moment was such that on the 11th December 1945 the new Kurdish national flag was hoisted in the town. Then, despite cautious advice from the Soviet Union, on the 22nd January 1946 Kurdish independence was proclaimed to an assembly of Kurds and townspeople by Qazi Mohammed (who was wearing a Soviet-type uniform and his religious head-dress) in the

---

[1] Not to be confused with the later Kurdistan Democratic Party, or the Democratic Party Kurdistan, the DPK, as it became known and which emerged in January 1960.

Chwar Chira (Four Lamps), an open square in the town of Mahabad. The new state was to be known as the Republic of Mahabad. On the 11th February 1946 Qazi Mohammed was appointed President. An attempt was made to bring in individuals from all over Kurdish territory, especially from Turkey and Iraq, so that a cabinet could be broadly representative of the race, but this was not successful. The majority of the Government and its officials were drawn from Mahabad and the Kurdish areas under Soviet occupation; the Persian Army severely discouraged any participation below the Sardasht–Saqqiz line. Although there were a few outsiders in the new Government, it could not be said that it fairly represented Greater Kurdistan by any means. The writ of the new Republic ran only to about fifty miles or so from Mahabad town, where work on organizing a government, a government service and an army began.

Two virtually independent states, almost side by side and traditionally hostile towards each other, had suddenly come into being, which was rather more than the Soviet Union had planned for. The Azerbaijani state demanded that the Kurdish one should come under its control, but the Kurds refused even to consider the proposal. There were also disputes over tracts of territory between the two, ownership being claimed by both over what was still virtually a 'no-man's-land'. The Soviet Union wanted the two states to merge into one bloc, become Sovietized and then agitate for incorporation into the Soviet Union, but it had not been able to do enough ground work in the time available. Britain had already evacuated its troops from Persia and world opinion was pressing for the Soviet Union to fulfil the terms of the wartime Tripartite Treaty and do likewise. With their political tasks hardly begun, the Russians were loath to leave.

The only means of defence possessed by the Mahabad Republic were the groups of armed followers of the various tribal sheikhs who had promised allegiance. As these were mercurial and of doubtful reliability, the new Government was determined to have a regular standing army, so as to be independent of tribal whims, and a Soviet officer was sent to form and train it. Towards the end of February 1946 two more consignments of Soviet arms, believed to amount to 5,000 rifles and pistols, a few machine-guns, and a quantity of ammunition and petrol bombs (Molotov cocktails), were received at Mahabad, but there was no sign of a promised delivery of tanks or artillery or, indeed, of any financial assistance. The Army also received a few Soviet and American trucks and jeeps. At its maximum strength the

Mahabad Republic's Army[1] consisted of 70 officers, 40 non-commissioned officers and 1,200 Sarbaz (privates). Most of the officers and senior ranks had served in either the Persian or Iraqi Armies or the British-sponsored Iraq Levies, and so had some experience. Many of the officers were taken away to undertake essential governmental or administrative jobs, and so the tiny force was under-officered all the time. Remaining in or near Mahabad, the Army never achieved any great degree of effectiveness; it was actually something in the nature of a presidential guard for the Mahabad Government, its main tasks being guard and escort duties. The defence of the Republic continued to rest in the hands of the tribal sheikhs who could muster groups of fighting men. On the 31st March 1946 the Mahabad Government appointed four generals, one of whom was Mullah Mustafa (an appointment he proudly retains to this day). The Government granted military ranks and titles sparsely, the few recipients of honorary distinctions being important sheikhs with a military following. Soon the Army, members of the Government and officials were clad in Soviet-type uniforms.

Early in March Mullah Mustafa brought more armed followers into Mahabad until there were over 3,000 Barzanis in the town. Thus he demonstrated his military power as his was by far the largest and best disciplined of all the Kurdish contingents, and it overawed the newly forming Mahabad regular Army. The Barzanis were on their best behaviour and kept to themselves, but neither they nor Mullah Mustafa were completely trusted. Lobbying hard, Mullah Mustafa tried to convince the Soviet authorities that he was the man they should choose to head the new Kurdish Republic, and that they should back him rather than Qazi Mohammed, but he had little success. However, at the same time Mullah Mustafa kept a close and overtly friendly contact with the President, Qazi Mohammed. It was because of his large military contingent that Mullah Mustafa had been given the rank of general and that he was treated with such respect.

Both the Mahabad and Azerbaijan republics were in an aggressive, expansionist mood, although they knew that when the Soviet occupation troops, under whose protective cloak they had come into being and continued to exist, were withdrawn they would have to face the Persian Army, which was already moving troops up to the Sardasht–Zanjan Line, ready to advance northwards to regain control of all

[1] According to Eagleton in *The Kurdish Republic*.

Persian territory. In March 1946 a tribal group of Kurds had made an unsuccessful raid on Persian outposts near Sardasht. In April the Azerbaijan Republic partisans commenced to occupy all population centres on the fringe and border areas between the Azerbaijan and the Mahabad republics, including the town of Rezaieh. On the 9th May 1946 the last Soviet troops were withdrawn from Persian soil, and the two new republics were left alone, callously abandoned by their sponsor, to defend themselves as best they could. There were now two military threats to the Mahabad Republic, one from the Azerbaijan Republic and the other from the Persian Army, the latter having mustered about 13,000 soldiers in the region of the Saqqiz–Sardasht Line. The Mahabad Republic kept its tiny regular army at home, and did its best to persuade those sheikhs with armed tribesmen to rush off to defend the vaguely defined frontiers. Mullah Mustafa and his Barzanis were given about 1,200 small arms, and early in April they moved off southwards to an area just north of Saqqiz, while smaller contingents of the Shikak and Herki tribes went to the area just to the north of Baneh. Estimates of numbers vary considerably. Probably there were about 12,000 armed tribesmen giving some sort of allegiance to the Mahabad Republic. Their capabilities and value varied immensely, but most set off, mainly in small groups under their own sheikhs, for the frontier areas where the threats lay.

On the 24th April a small Persian force advanced northwards from Saqqiz, only to be ambushed by the Barzanis and driven back again. Some Persian prisoners were taken and sent off to Mahabad. This successful action was extremely good for the Barzanis' morale, and gave them great prestige throughout the new republic; so much confidence did it engender that the Mahabad Government began to formulate plans for a Kurdish advance southwards to occupy all Kurdish territory in Persia. The Barzanis were in positions in the mountains overlooking the roads from Saqqiz to both Baneh and Sardasht, all three places having Persian garrisons, and so they were able to block Persian communications. On the 3rd May an impromptu agreement was made by local Persian Army commanders and the Barzanis allowing the Kurds to pull back a little way to let the Persians have access to their beleaguered garrisons. This was not well received in Mahabad, as the Government, still intoxicated with its grand strategy of sweeping south to occupy all Kurdish territory, intended to concentrate its forces at Saqqiz, preparatory to advancing

53

on Sanandaj.[1] During late May and early June the Barzanis crept back into their former positions, from where they could once again snipe at Persian military traffic on the roads below. On the 13th June a Persian force over 2,000 strong, with aircraft, tanks and artillery in support, moved out from Saqqiz to attack the Mamashah Heights, a few miles to the north-west, which were held by a handful of Barzanis. After a stiff resistance all day, the Heights were finally taken by the Persians, but while they thereby gained considerable tactical advantages, the Barzanis were able to turn their defeat into a minor military epic. Barzani fighting stock, always high, rose to a new peak.

After this engagement, truce talks began on the Persian front and dragged on while the fighting lapsed. Differences were arising between tribal Kurds and urbanized Kurds, many of the latter being in influential positions in the Mahabad Government. As a result several of the smaller tribes withdrew their fighting contingents from the forward areas, especially from the Persian front, which by this time was most decidedly the most dangerous. The gaps caused were filled by Barzanis, who practically took over the defence of the whole front, ranging from Sardasht to Baneh, which gave Mullah Mustafa more prestige and influence. Soviet advisers voiced doubts to the Mahabad Government on the loyalty, or continued loyalty, of many of the Kurdish sheikhs, and there were differences of opinion as to whether the Azerbaijan front should be given greater or less priority than the Persian front.

On the 19th July cavalry elements of the Shikak and Herki tribes advanced towards the town of Maku, near the Soviet frontier, and also towards the town of Khei, to the north-east of Lake Rezaieh, but the Azerbaijan Republic sent detachments of its armed forces against them and the Kurds withdrew. Meanwhile, the Soviet Union, which was now more interested in gaining Persian oil concessions, had persuaded the Mahabad Government to abandon all thoughts of a Kurdish offensive southwards. In August Qazi Mohammed went to Teheran to try to negotiate with the Persian Government, but it was deeply involved in a power struggle with the Tudeh Party. On the 19th October a new Government was formed in Persia which contained no Tudeh ministers; its policy was vigorously to restore full governmental control over the whole of the country. Determined military action, first of all aimed at the Azerbaijan Republic, was initiated. By the 16th November Persian troops were back in Zanjan,

[1] Formerly Senna.

and on the 13th December Government forces entered Tabriz, when the Azerbaijan Republic collapsed completely.

In the meantime the Kurdish tribes, quarrelling amongst themselves when they realized there was no prospect of loot, began to desert the Mahabad Republic. On the 11th December 1946 the Shikak and Herki tribes moved off towards Tabriz. After withdrawing from the Persian front the Barzanis went first of all to Mahabad, with the overt intention of defending that town but, seeing that the military situation was hopeless, Mullah Mustafa led them in early December to the Naqadeh area, near the corner of Iraq. Thus Mahabad was virtually left defenceless, with only its tiny and indifferent army, obviously incapable of resisting the Persian forces.

On the 16th December 1946 Qazi Mohammed went to Miandoab and surrendered to the Persian authorities. The following day Persian troops entered Mahabad, to be formally welcomed by Qazi Mohammed himself: it was the end of the short-lived Kurdish Mahabad Republic. Later, on the 31st March 1947, Qazi Mohammed and three other prominent Kurdish leaders were hanged at Mahabad. The Republic, the first Kurdish one, had had an unfortunate existence; its birth was rushed and its death came quickly. Once the Soviet Union withdrew its troops, the Republic never had a chance. It was only after considerable hesitation that the Soviet Union backed it in the first instance, and then its support was barely lukewarm, as it had really wanted the Kurds to merge into Persian Azerbaijan. The Soviet Union had given little, except a few small arms and a set of military band instruments. The promised financial backing did not materialize, and the Mahabad Republic remained solvent only by selling its tobacco crop at a low price to the Soviet Union in May 1946.

The well-armed Barzanis sat sullenly in the mountainous Naqadeh area, from where it would obviously require a major campaign on the part of the Persian Army to dislodge them, so Mullah Mustafa went to Teheran to try to negotiate terms with the Government. He spent a month there without reaching any agreement. The Persian Government offered to allow the Barzanis to settle around Mount Alvand, near Hamadan, if they would hand in their arms, and although Mullah Mustafa was in favour, his brother, Sheikh Ahmed, refused the offer, so it was not taken up. Mullah Mustafa said he would return to Barzan if either the British or Iraqi Governments would guarantee his safety, but this did not come to anything either.

The Persian Government mounted a large expedition against the Barzanis, in which troops were well supported by aircraft, which drove Mullah Mustafa farther into the mountains. Persian troops entered Naqadeh on the 22nd February 1947. Next, the Persians incited the tribal enemies of the Barzanis to move against them in conjunction with the Army, and during March and April the Barzanis were pressed on land and harried from the air. Several small actions were fought in which Persian troops suffered casualties. This continual harassment was a great strain on the Barzanis, who had their families with them, and it caused internal dissension. Mullah Mustafa was all in favour of holding out and fighting on, but he gradually came to be in the minority as morale drooped, the majority wanting to return to their tribal homes around Barzan almost at any price. On the 25th April 1947 Mullah Mustafa took them back across the border into Iraq with the intention of submitting to the authorities. Almost at once several leaders were arrested, and the whole tribe was put under strict supervision. Four were executed in June, but Mullah Mustafa and a number of his followers managed to evade the Iraqi authorities, although Sheikh Ahmed, his elder brother, surrendered to them. Mullah Mustafa alleges that at this period he was invited to go to Britain, but instead chose to try to fight his way through to the Soviet Union, his reason being that Britain was much too far away from Kurdish territory.

Commencing his fighting retreat on the 27th May 1947 with 496 followers, Mullah Mustafa moved north from the Barzan area and then cut across the north-east corner of Turkey, moving to the west of Mount Dalanpur on the border, before crossing the mountains back into Persia. He then travelled due north, keeping to the west of Lake Rezaieh, through the territory of the hostile Mamash tribe (estimated to be 12,000 strong) to cross the Aras River, near Mount Ararat. He entered Soviet territory on the 15th June 1947 where, accepted by the Soviet authorities, he remained for eleven years. Following him, Persian army units moved up to the Soviet border and consolidated their grip on Kurdish territory, while the Iraqis also clamped down on the Kurds in their country. So sadly ended the first Kurdish Republic, and the fighting in which the Barzanis had played the predominant part. Mullah Mustafa, who with others was condemned to death in his absence in Iraq, had gained a reputation as an active Kurdish nationalist leader.

3

KURDISH NATIONALISM REVIVED

'There is no Kurdish problem when a Turkish bayonet appears.'

Ghassemlou

During the decade after 1947 the Kurds in Turkey and Persia were largely disarmed and brought sharply to heel. Those in Iraq were allowed to retain their arms and were able to maintain a degree of independence from governmental control. It was a decade in which Kurdish nationalism languished, in which there were only minor tribal disorders, but it was followed by a revival of Kurdish discontent in Iraq and a revolt in Turkey. In Iraq, by mid-1961, Kurdish rebellion was close to the surface.

In Persia, as soon as the campaign against the republics of Mahabad and Azerbaijan was completed, the Government set about systematically disarming the Kurdish tribesmen. The first to be dealt with were those living around Mahabad. Kurdish nationalist organizations were suppressed, and Soviet radio propaganda and subversive pamphlets in the Kurdish language failed to stimulate the Kurds, who had little in common with the Russians, into insurrection. After a while these repressive measures were relaxed somewhat, perhaps because they were largely unenforceable, especially in regard to wearing Kurdish dress, using the Kurdish language and carrying arms. However, the Kurds in Persia had been badly shaken by World War II. For example,[1] 'Of the 10,000 members of the Talili tribe (that lived near the borders of the USSR and Turkey) deported to the central areas of Iran, only a few hundred returned in 1941, all the rest having died.' With the assistance of an American military mission the Persian Army was reorganized, and by about 1962 its strength had risen to approximately 208,000 (conscription being in force for a two-year period) disposed into some twelve divisions, with artillery and some Soviet T–34 and American M–47 tanks. Additionally there was a para-military gendarmerie of 30,000. The Air Force, with a strength of some 7,500 men, had about 150 air-

[1] Ghassemlou.

57

craft, that included F–84 Thunderjets, F–86 Sabrejets and FD–47 Thunderbolts: another 100 US aircraft were on order. Soon the Persian Government was insisting, with a great deal of truth, that it did not have a Kurdish problem. However, the illegal Democratic Party of Kurdistan continued to exist underground, but it was cautious and moderate in its views and comments.

During the existence of the Mahabad Republic in Persia, the Kurds in Iraq had remained comparatively quiet, despite exhortations to revolt and join in the fight for a Greater Kurdistan. The only clash of note occurred when an Iraqi Army column had to be sent to the Sinjar area in Mosul province. In 1947, as the defeated Barzanis trickled back over the border into Iraq, they were dispossessed of their property, many were arrested and others placed under house arrest. Property and land taken from the Barzanis was given out to the Kurdish tribes that had fought for the Government against them. Most of the Kurds in Iraq, including the Barzanis, were permitted to retain their arms.

Early in 1947 hostilities bubbled up between a group of Barzanis and the Jaf tribe, which lived to the south of Suleimaniya, near the Persian border, while Iraqi troops remained in Barzan because of the subversive activities of another group of Barzanis, led by Mohammed Khalid, son of old Sheikh Ahmed Barzani. Throughout the year there was an uneasy and uncertain situation between the Pishdaris, who lived to the north-east of Suleimaniya, and the Piranis, who inhabited an area near Arbil. The Barzanis soon found means to obtain more arms.

During 1948 there were strikes and riots in Baghdad, some of which called for the release of Kurdish leaders from prison. In September 1950 Nuri Said toured Kurdish territory, made a few vague promises, and slightly eased restrictions on tribal movement and surveillance; in the following year programmes in the Kurdish language were broadcast from Radio Baghdad. Otherwise, despite the Kurds' deep divisions amongst themselves, their antipathy towards the Arab Iraqi Government, and the virulent propaganda from the Soviet Union, Kurdish territory remained passive, mainly, perhaps, because no leader of any stature and reputation remained at liberty. Sheikh Mahmoud Barzanji had returned from exile to die, in 1956, at Nasiriya. Mullah Mustafa was in the Soviet Union and Sheikh Ahmed was under arrest.

Although they were little more than pale shadows, one or two

Kurdish nationalist organizations remained in existence under-ground, but they were very chastened and spent their efforts in maintaining themselves, asserting themselves and trying to wrest the leadership from the tribal sheikhs—a tussle that went on for some time and which in 1948 led to scuffles in the streets of Suleimaniya. There was a wide gap between the tribal Kurds in the mountains and the detribalized Kurds in the towns and cities. The Iraqi Communist Party, itself splintered and shaky, swung what weight it could on the side of the Kurdish nationalists against traditional conservatism.

By 1943 the Iraqi Army had run right down; out of an establishment of some 30,000, over 20,000 had 'disappeared', and the police were forbidden to trace and apprehend deserters. With British help it was in 1944 revived and reorganized, but two years later, when it was required to stand by for possible trouble in Kurdish territory, it was still in a comparatively poor condition, its soldiers having low pay, inadequate rations and insufficient equipment. Still led mainly by Turkish-trained officers, it had done no serious training for years. An officer's appointment was regarded as a sinecure, and many were content with that. In time the standard of the junior officers slowly rose, but in general the senior officers remained ever-interested in politics and lacked respect for the democratic principle that the military must always be subordinate to the civil power.

Remembering the Rashid Ali coup of 1941, Nuri Said did not want the Army to become too strong, although he relied upon it for much of his support and it was essential to maintain internal security; but plans were made for it to consist ultimately of three infantry and one armoured division. By 1948 when, short of adequate equipment, it briefly intervened without any particular honour or effectiveness in the Arab–Israeli War, it consisted of some twelve brigades. A force of 12,000 men in trucks, under General Saleh Saib, had crossed from Trans-Jordan into Palestine. Dissatisfied with the quantity of British equipment supplied after 1948, the Iraqi Army tried unsuccessfully to obtain American arms and military material.[1] By 1956 the force consisted of about fourteen brigades, of which perhaps only four infantry and two armoured were capable of taking the field. By this time its strength had risen to about 60,000 men. Conscription for a two-year period was in force, but there were many exemptions. Iraq was short of trucks and vehicles and its grandiose plan to make the

---

[1] The last remaining British troops left Iraq in October 1947, only RAF personnel remaining at Habbaniya.

whole army completely mobile had not progressed far. The RAF had helped to rebuild the Iraqi Air Force, which by 1956 had some 250 aircraft, mainly British types and some quite modern. There were also about 20,000 armed police, of whom about 6,000 formed a mobile force, stationed in the capital.

In 1954 political parties were allowed to appear openly, to form briefly what was known as the National Front, and to take part in the general election of that year, which was won by Nuri Said and his Constitutional Union Party. In fact, the National Front contained the Baathists, the Istaqlal, the National Democrats and the Communists. The Baathi Party of Iraq had just been formed as a regional off-shoot from the main Baathist Party of Syria, which regarded it as subordinate. Its platform was a mixture of revolutionary nationalism and socialism. The Istaqlal (Independence) Party had been formed in 1946, with the original aim of eliminating British influence, and it was extremely nationalistic. The National Democratic Party, also formed in 1946, was slightly left-wing, advocating liberal reforms. In the early 1950s the Iraqi Communist Party splintered, but the several pieces came together again for the election period. Although illegal, the ICP had been able to work almost openly through some of its 'front organizations'.

After the election Nuri Said banned all political parties again, and the Kurdish nationalist organizations in particular were harshly repressed. The National Front continued to exist underground until 1958, thus ensuring some liaison between the various parties. Although Nuri Said himself was not anti-Kurdish—he was mainly indifferent—his Arab ministers were, and they all leaned heavily against any tendency towards autonomy or fragmentation of the country. Nuri Said was in fact pro-Western and anti-Communist, and indeed had been waging almost a personal cold war against the Soviet Union. In 1955 he negotiated the Baghdad Pact, which tied Iraq to the West, against Arab opposition both in Iraq and elsewhere in the Middle East. The Pact enabled the Iraqi armed forces to obtain a little more, but not much, military material from Western sources.

In 1954, when it was seen that most of the earlier Kurdish nationalist organizations had either disintegrated or lost their potency, the United Democratic Party of Kurdistan (UDPK) rose from the ashes of the Kurdistan Democratic Party, which had been formed in August 1946 from the remains of the old Heva when that dissolved. The members of the UDPK consisted mainly of detribalized Kurds living in the cities and towns, its branches becoming quite strong in Baghdad, Mosul, Kirkuk and Basra, all of which had mixed populations. Although professing vague Marxist-Leninist ideas, the UDPK concerned itself primarily with Kurdish problems, but its demands at this stage were moderate and never did it mention autonomy or independence. The Secretary of the UDPK was Ibrahim Ahmed, a Communist lawyer from Suleimaniya who had been first appointed Secretary of the KDP in 1952, after serving a prison sentence for political offences, and the absent Mullah Mustafa Barzani was nominated Chairman apparently without his knowledge or consent.[1] The UDPK came to have a Central Committee of twenty-one members, and an inner Politburo of five, who initially were Ibrahim Ahmed, Jelal Talabani, Omar Mustafa, Nuri Sadik Showais and Ali Abdullah. The UDPK maintained close contact with the reviving ICP.

His pro-Western and anti-Nasser views made Nuri Said extremely unpopular in many quarters, and at the time of the Anglo-French attack on Egypt in 1956 there were demonstrations against him in Baghdad, but he declared martial law and kept Iraq in the Baghdad Pact. Nuri Said's rivalry with President Nasser became more acute and bitter; when on the 14th February 1958 the United Arab Republic, consisting of Egypt and Syria, came into being, Nuri Said worked for the union of Iraq and Jordan as a counter. He had always had visions of a federation of Fertile Crescent countries, and when he won the election in May 1958 it was expected that this would become a reality. Another cause of his unpopularity was that he resisted all proposals to tax the land-owning sheikhs, who were his main props. A number of clandestine organizations were plotting against Nuri Said, but most of them were relatively ineffectual, the exception being the Free Officers Movement, which had come into being in 1952, having mushroomed into life in various garrisons more or less spontaneously. These elements gradually fused, and the Suez War of 1956 accelerated this process. The Free Officers Central Committee, the chairman of which was Brigadier Abdul Karim Kassem, then commanding the 19th Infantry Brigade stationed at Bakuba, worked to bring all groups under its direction. Kassem, born in 1914, was commissioned in the Iraqi Army in 1934, attended the Iraqi Staff College in 1941, took a senior officers course in Britain in 1950, and was promoted brigadier in 1955. He had joined the Free Officers Movement in 1954.

---

[1] Sometimes referred to as the President at this period.

One Iraqi brigade was already in Jordan to bolster up that country's Government. Another, the 20th, stationed at Jalaula, some 90 miles to the north-west of Baghdad, was ordered to move to Jordan to reinforce it in case of a coup against the projected union of Iraq and Jordan. To get there it had to stage at the capital. The Free Officers chose this moment to seize power. In the early hours of the 14th July 1958, in the name of the Free Officers, Colonel Abdul Salim Aref took over command of the 20th Infantry Brigade, marched it into Baghdad, and with the assistance of strategically placed Free Officers, he secured by dawn the army camps and key points, gaining the adherence of the units in the capital. When the police were dominated, the Free Officers moved against the Royal Palace, which was bombarded; Colonel Aref incited the mob to join in the attack. After brief resistance the Palace Guards surrendered. King Feisal and Prince Abdul Illah, the Regent, were arrested and executed, their bodies being mutilated and publicly exhibited. Kassem meanwhile had brought his 19th Infantry Brigade into Baghdad, while Nuri Said, the Premier, was caught after several days in hiding and lynched by a mob. The régime of Nuri Said had come to a violent end, but it was later stated by Kassem that only nineteen people were killed in this coup.

Brigadier Kassem became Premier, Minister of Defence and Minister of the Interior, and Colonel Aref became the Deputy Premier. Apart from three Free Officers in the first Kassem Cabinet, nine of the thirteen members were civilians, and included representatives of the Baathist Party, the Istaqlal, the National Democratic Party and the UDPK, but no Communists. Kassem obviously wished to gain as wide support as possible. The Kurd was Baba Ali, who became Minister of Communications. A Sovereignty Council of three was formed, to which another Kurd, Khalid Naqshabandi, was appointed. The projected union of Iraq and Jordan was dropped, the Iraqi brigade returned from the country, and diplomatic contacts were made with some Communist countries, including the Soviet Union. Kassem promoted himself major-general,[1] retired all officers above the rank of brigadier, and replaced them with his nominees. In retrospect, the Kurds claimed they were the deciding factor that brought Kassem to power, but this claim cannot be substantiated. Strong evidence suggests that Kassem's mother was a Kurd, but he denied it, publicly stating that she was an Arab. In an effort to unify

[1] Kassem promoted himself lieutenant-general on the 6th January 1963.

62

his country, Kassem tried to be all things to all men, to bring together in harmony not only the political parties and the Shias and Sunnis, but also the races, the Arabs, Kurds and Assyrians. Needing the support of the Kurds, just after the coup he released a number of Kurdish leaders amid much publicity, but he reminded them that the Kurds were part of the Iraqi nation. On the 17th July Ibrahim Ahmed, Secretary of the UDPK, led a delegation to Kassem, asking for a degree of autonomy, but this request was refused. However, as a gesture of good will Kassem released Sheikh Ahmed from arrest. The new Provisional Constitution, announced on the 27th July, stated that 'Arabs and Kurds were considered partners in the homeland . . . [that] . . . their national rights within Iraqi sovereignty were recognized'—but it went no further. This principle came to be referred to as the 'partnership of Arabs and Kurds', an expression that was bandied about for a while.

During his exile in the Soviet Union, Mullah Mustafa Barzani had visited Moscow and Baku, but attempts to indoctrinate him had not made any deep impression. In July 1958 Mullah Mustafa was in Prague, and after the Iraqi coup he and Kassem exchanged messages, but Kassem remained non-committal for a while. It was not until the 3rd September that he pardoned all concerned with the postwar Barzani insurrections, when Mullah Mustafa, still nominally the Chairman of the UDPK, was formally invited to return to Iraq. Although Mullah Mustafa wanted the freedom to return to Iraq at this juncture, he was not keen to become involved with the UDPK, so he prevaricated—hence the delay. However, he was 'co-opted' by the Politburo of the UDPK as its nominal leader, as it wanted to draw on the strength of his reputation amongst the Kurds. It needed, too, his tribal bases and support. Kassem made it a condition of his return that he accept this position.[1] The UDPK Politburo obviously hoped that his stay in the Soviet Union had communized Mullah Mustafa, and at least made him susceptible to Communist influences and ideas. Ibrahim Ahmed, with a delegation, left Iraq to escort Mullah Mustafa back home. After stopping off at Cairo for an interview with President Nasser, he arrived in Baghdad on the 6th October. Mullah Mustafa's meeting with Kassem was reported to have been cordial, but when Kassem wanted Mullah Mustafa to forgive his Kurdish enemies he was not willing to go as far as that. For some

[1] 'I was forced to become President (of the UDPK) by Kassem,' according to David Adamson.

time Mullah Mustafa remained in Baghdad, under scarcely veiled house arrest, being only allowed brief visits to the mountains. Meanwhile, on the 19th August, Ibrahim Ahmed had asked permission of Abdul Salim Aref, the Deputy Premier, to publish a UDPK newspaper. This had been refused, as had a request from the Kurds to have their Nowruz (new year's festival), on the 21st March officially recognized as a holiday. Mullah Mustafa's followers who had been with him in the Soviet Union swelled in number to 850; they were embarked on a Soviet ship, which eventually landed them at Basra, to arrive in Baghdad on the 16th April 1959 to a hero's welcome. The increase in number was not clearly explained, but the original group may have been joined by other Kurdish refugees and local Soviet Kurds deliberately fed in by the Russians.

Some Kurdish tribes, especially the traditional enemies of the Barzanis, were uneasy at the return of Mullah Mustafa and at having to give back the Barzanis' confiscated land and property they had previously been awarded for fighting for the Government against them. In November 1958 there were discontented rumblings in the mountains, mainly against Mullah Mustafa and the UDPK. Within the UDPK there was a certain amount of friction and animosity between Mullah Mustafa and Ibrahim Ahmed, the Secretary, but they worked together because Ibrahim Ahmed realized that Mullah Mustafa was the only prestige personality available who could command sufficient Kurdish respect and some tribal power—the UDPK still had practically no impact on the mountain tribesmen as a whole.

On the 1st August 1958 Kassem began the Popular Resistance Force movement to defend the Revolution, which came to contain a large element of peasants from the southern, poorer parts of Iraq. The PRF formed its own militia, that included women as well as men, and soon it was reported that over 20,000 were undergoing training. The Communists took a prominent part in this organization and in leading this militia. By January 1959 the PRF militia was virtually controlling the streets of Baghdad, and even making its own political arrests, a situation that caused Kassem to utter warnings. As a precaution Kassem formed a fifth division, to be based in the capital, which really consisted only of the former Royal Guards and some other units brought into Baghdad. All the personnel had, however, been carefully screened for their loyalty to him. In Kurdish territory the PRF militia was dominated by the followers of Mullah Mustafa, who had been in exile with him in the Soviet Union; under their direction it began to terrorize local landowners, who became alarmed at its left-wing policies. Its influence grew until in certain sectors it replaced the police and frontier guards. After loud protests from the tribal sheikhs, PRF activities were suspended in Kurdish territory, officially on the 14th January 1959, but Kassem, Mullah Mustafa and Ibrahim Ahmed realized that they were pushing socialism too fast.

In September 1958 Abdul Salim Aref toured Kurdish territory, promising reforms and speaking of redistribution of land, which upset the sheikhs and landowners and also most of the tribal Kurds as well, who feared they might be merged into the larger Arab element in Iraq. Shortly after this Aref was successively relieved of his posts and responsibilities, and sent as Ambassador to Germany. When he returned to Iraq without permission, he was arrested, tried and imprisoned.

Since the 1958 coup certain political parties had come into the open, but the UDPK was still not permitted to operate without restriction. The party that seemed to gain the most influence in the first months of Kassem's régime was the ICP, which had many Kurdish members, its Secretary, for example, being Khalid Bakdash, a Kurd from Damascus. The UDPK, with a membership mainly of detribalized Kurds, most of whom were in sympathy with Communist ideals, invariably followed the ICP line in all but Kurdish matters, and so the two parties at this stage were extremely close together. After some argument over the phrase 'Kurdish self-determination', which had to be struck out, a Covenant of Co-operation between the ICP and the UDPK was signed on the 10th November 1958. It was the secret Communist plan to infiltrate first of all into the UDPK, seize key positions, and then take it over completely and merge it into the ICP.

When they had come out into the open after the 1958 coup, the National Democratic Party, the Istaqlal Party and the Baathists severed their connexion with the Communists, thus breaking up the National Front, which had survived in a fragile underground form since 1954. However, the National Front was revived on the 23rd November 1958, when the National Democratic Party, the Istaqlal Party and the ICP came together again, agreeing to work for Iraqi independence and Arab solidarity. This time the Baathists were left out.

There was a vociferous element in Iraq that demanded the union

E   65

of Iraq with Nasser's UAR, which was contrary to Kassem's view. The suppression of a plot against him was announced on the 7th December 1958; it involved Rashid Ali Gailani, the former anti-British Premier of 1941 notoriety, who was a Nasserite.[1] After the failure of this plot, Kassem broke with President Nasser, and as a counter to the pro-Nasser factions in Iraq he turned to the Communists for support. The winter of 1958–9 saw the rapid growth of Communist influence; in particular the Communists infiltrated the PRF movement and militia, the trade unions and the student organizations. Reshuffling his Cabinet in February 1959, Kassem included more left-wing members so as to be able to resist demands to join the UAR. This Cabinet contained two Kurds, Hasan Talabani and Fuad Aref.

The next event of importance in Iraq was the Mosul mutiny of March 1959, when on the 6th of that month several thousand Communist-inspired Partisans of Peace held a rally in Mosul, a city with a mixed population of Turkomans,[2] Assyrians, Kurds and Arabs, amounting to some 350,000—the majority of the oil-workers were Kurds. That day and the next the pro-Communist demonstrators clashed with the Assyrians and Moslems, causing Colonel Shawaf, the anti-Communist garrison commander, to impose a curfew and make arrests. A kidnapped British engineer was made to work his radio transmitter, and on the 8th Colonel Shawaf, who was in favour of union with the UAR, announced his intention of marching on Baghdad to seize power. It was later alleged that Colonel Shawaf had the support and encouragement of the local landowners, and that he was also given some help by Nasser, who persuaded the Shammar, an Arab tribe which occupied an area from just west of Mosul right into Syria, to march on that town. The rebels made a brief, pathetic attempt to bomb Radio Baghdad, and anarchy broke out in the streets of Mosul. Kassem's reply was an ultimatum to surrender. Mullah Mustafa came out on Kassem's side and called upon the Kurds to rise against Colonel Shawaf, while the Communists urged the PRF to do likewise.

On the 9th Iraqi aircraft bombed Colonel Shawaf's headquarters, wounding him. He was taken to hospital, where he was killed by an

[1] The 'Nasserites' were generally associated with the Arab Nationalist Movement, the ANM, a pan-Arab one active in several countries, which recognized Nasser as the leader of the Arab socialist revolution.

[2] An expression used to embrace Turks and those of Turkish descent living outside the boundaries of present-day Turkey.

officer loyal to Kassem. Anarchy in Mosul increased as the PRF militia, supported by local Kurds in the city, attacked the rebels and the Shammar tribesmen who were arriving. Shooting and looting occurred, many atrocities were committed—especially against pro-Nasser officers—and the Shammar leader was killed. It was not until the 10th, when other Iraqi Army units arrived, that order was restored in Mosul. No reliable casualty figures were issued, but it was estimated that some 2,000 people had lost their lives. As the mountain Kurds approached in force, their traditional enemies, the Shammar,[1] faded away and withdrew into Syrian territory. They abandoned arms, which were seized by both Kurds and the PRF militia, who also took and kept arms from killed or captured rebels or those who surrendered. After being severely restricted in its activities three months earlier, the Communist-dominated PRF in Mosul once again came into full prominence. Colonel Shawaf had hardly any practical support in Iraq, apart from an attempted rising at Arbil, which was crushed almost as soon as it started, and another at Akda, a Kurdish area, which also failed.

An event of major importance in Iraq was the Kirkuk massacre in which over 120 people[2] were killed and over 100 wounded. Kassem arrested six officers and about 250 soldiers, and dismissed some 800 reserve officers, because he thought they had been influenced by Communists during their training. On the 14th July 1959, the anniversary of the Kassem coup, fighting broke out in the streets of Kirkuk, the oil town, between Turkomans and Kurds, in which the Communist-led PRF became involved. Army units were ordered to intervene, but as the majority of the soldiers were Kurds many refused to obey orders, and indeed numbers joined with their compatriots in fighting the other factions. There was a lack of definite army leadership at this moment, as the pro-Communist commander of the 2nd Infantry Division, which garrisoned the region, had just been dismissed. For three days there was anarchy, until by the 17th the Communists had gained control of Kirkuk. Order was only finally restored on the 18th, when army units from Baghdad, under the command of Colonel Abdul Rahman Aref (brother of the imprisoned Abdul Salim Aref), arrived to take over. Kassem blamed

---

[1] Members of the Shammar tribe involved were amnestied on the 7th April 1959 by Kassem.
[2] Kassem admitted that 79 had been killed, including 40 buried alive and 140 injured.

the Communists, and produced plans to show that they intended to assassinate certain political leaders, including Mullah Mustafa Barzani. The ICP headquarters at Kirkuk was closed down and the PRF militia ceased training.

After the Kirkuk massacre Communist influence in Iraq declined rapidly as Kassem, to counter it, released batches of political prisoners, but it had really been on the wane since 29th April 1959, when Kassem had refused an ICP request for representation in the Government. Already Kassem was becoming alarmed at the potential of Communist power, which was outgrowing that of any other party or faction. In June he refused the ICP demand that the National Front be activated in its former mould, claiming that it had the full support of the UDPK in this. On the 5th July the whole of the PRF militia was placed under the control of army officers, and on the 13th Kassem reshuffled his Cabinet, still without Communist representation. The Kirkuk incident had blown up the following day.

During 1959 Kassem completely eliminated any remaining power possessed by the Free Officers, who had brought him to office, by removing and retiring individuals. Other events of some political importance during the year included the withdrawal of Iraq from the Baghdad Pact[1] on the 4th April. On the same day the UDPK was allowed to publish its newspaper, *Khabat*, and other Kurdish language periodicals followed. Under Mullah Mustafa's guidance, although resisted by Ibrahim Ahmed, the UDPK—still in open accord with Kassem—drew away from the ICP, and when Kassem made his final break with the Communists in July the UDPK suspended those of its members who had signed the Covenant of Co-operation of November 1958. On the 6th January 1960 Kassem once again permitted certain political parties to operate legally, but this did not include the ICP, and although some Communist 'front organizations' existed, he again refused the request of the ICP in the following month to be recognized. The UDPK was one of the accepted parties, but it had to change its title slightly to that of the Kurdish Democratic Party, or the Democratic Party Kurdistan, the DPK. Kassem wanted the title to have a regional rather than an international character. Membership of the DPK gave the right to carry firearms, not normally permitted to the detribalized Kurds in the cities and towns.

---

[1] Renamed the Central Treaty Organization, CENTO, on the 21st August 1959, when its headquarters moved to Ankara.

Soon after he had returned from the Soviet Union, Mullah Mustafa tried to organize an international Kurdish congress, to be attended by Kurdish leaders not only from Iraq but also from Turkey, Persia, Syria and elsewhere, but he failed. The Kurds from Turkey and Persia were reluctant to become involved in anything of this nature, as it would be taken as a sign of political agitation against their respective governments and would attract punitive action. This failure to kindle a spark of international Kurdish support was a great disappointment both to Mullah Mustafa and the DPK, and also to the ICP, which had hoped somehow to be able to turn it to Communist advantage.

Kassem thought the Barzanis were becoming too powerful a faction within Iraq, and to reduce their influence he began playing the Kurdish tribes off against one another. At the same time, for instance, as the Kurds were holding their Fifth Kurdish Congress (from the 5th–10th May 1960), at which Mullah Mustafa was re-elected Chairman of the DPK, and Ibrahim Ahmed the Secretary, Kassem was receiving, with great publicity, deputations from the Surchi and Herki tribes, traditional enemies of the Barzanis, who had deliberately absented themselves from the Congress.

The DPK had become strongly infiltrated by Communists, and its Politburo was dominated by them. A purge begun on Mullah Mustafa's insistence lessened their influence; several were removed from positions of responsibility, including the Communist editor of *Khabat*, and all Communist references in the DPK constitution were struck out. There was still friction within the DPK, especially between Mullah Mustafa and Ibrahim Ahmed and their respective followings, and between Mullah Mustafa and former members of the old Heva and other old Kurdish nationalist groups, but even so, although many disliked Mullah Mustafa himself or his policies, they all supported him as the leader of the Kurdish nationalist cause. In November 1960 the Editor of *Khabat* was put on trial by the Government for stirring up national dissension, but he was acquitted. The same month the Kurdish language weekly in Kirkuk, *Deh Nagi Kurd*, was suspended for criticizing the authorities in that town.

In Persia, when Kassem came to power and Mullah Mustafa returned from the Soviet Union, the Government became anxious in case there should be sympathetic unrest in its Kurdish territory, but this did not occur and the mountain tribes remained quiet. By December 1959 relations between Iraq and Persia were deteriorating over conflicting claims concerning the Shatt-al-Arab. The Persian Kurds did not exploit this situation either.

In Turkey in 1958 and 1959 the 'Mountain Turks' remained quiet under the firm restraining hand of the Government, but the following year they took advantage of the political instability between the supporters of the 1960 Revolution and other rival political parties to agitate for Kurdish rights in the eastern vilayets, and there were disorders and demonstrations. On the 21st May 1960 the Democratic Party Government was overthrown[1] by the Turkish armed forces which then ruled the country through the Committee of the National Union, a body of military officers, until elections in October the following year, after which Turkey was ruled by a succession of coalition governments until the elections of 1965, when a unitary one was formed. However, despite internal political quarrels, the Turks momentarily forgot their feuds, and banded together to react unitedly and strongly against the insurgent Kurds. Extra army units moved into Kurdish territory, blocked off the border and then closed in on the dissidents, arresting and imprisoning many Kurdish leaders. Once this spasm of revolt was crushed, all was quiet again. In 1960 the population of Turkey was about 28 million, of whom only 3–4 million were Kurds, which meant they were a small, unpopular minority and could be dealt with harshly. With a standing army of some 500,000, composed of some twenty-two divisions and with a supporting air force with some 300 combat aircraft, the Turkish Government had the means to react with overpowering strength to any dissidence. Certain minor concessions made to the Kurds by the Menderes régime were cancelled by Premier Inonu.

The seemingly good relations between Mullah Mustafa, the ICP and Kassem disturbed some of the Kurdish tribes, especially those hostile to the Barzanis, as did the fact that sections of Kurdish tribal territory remained in the hands of the PRF militia, led by Soviet-trained followers of Mullah Mustafa. Although minor terrorist activities of the PRF during the autumn of 1958 had caused it to be nominally suspended on the 14th January 1959, it had regained control of a number of police and frontier posts. In April 1959, as soon as the receding snows allowed campaigning to begin again in the mountains, the Lolan tribe, under Sheikh Mohammed Rashid, attacked the PRF militia and drove it from the villages of Nabah and

[1] The Democratic Party Premier, Adnam Menderes, was executed on the 17th September 1961.

70

Kani. The Lolan tribe inhabited the area to the north-east of Ruwandiz. In retaliation, the Iraqi Government sent aircraft which bombed the Lolani villages with such intensity that the whole tribe, some 6,000 or more people, moved over the frontier into Turkey.

At the beginning of May the Pishdar tribe, led by Sheikh Abbas Mammand, which inhabited a large area to the north-east of Suleimaniya, took similar action against the PRF, occupying a number of police and frontier posts held by the Barzani-led militia. The weather was now more favourable and a combined operation by the Iraqi Air Force, Army, the PRF militia and the Barzanis, was mounted against the Pishdaris. The PRF militia refused to obey army orders, as did the Barzanis to a lesser extent, but such was the ferocity of the assaults that the whole of the Pishdar tribe, estimated to consist of about 20,000 people, crossed over the border into Persia, where they were put into camps by the Persian authorities for the time being.

Several other tribal sheikhs, notably those hostile to the Barzanis, became restless in the spring, but the treatment meted out to the Lolanis and Pishdaris caused them to restrain their followers. The lesson had not, however, been lost on Kassem. The PRF militia in tribal territory was placed under army officers, as it mainly was in the rest of Iraq. These brought it under control, and then some of its units were gradually disarmed and disbanded. Kassem granted amnesty to the Lolanis on the 25th June 1959, on condition that they returned to Iraq before the end of July. Most of them complied, being persuaded to do so by Sheikh Ahmed Barzani, who still had some influence with the tribes—mainly as a religious leader—and who remained friendly with Kassem.

Kassem now also fully appreciated the disruptive power of the Barzanis in tribal territory. He realized just how unpopular they were among the Kurdish tribes generally, so he intensified his efforts at playing them off against each other. He gave arms to the Lolanis, then to the Zibaris and the Baradostis, and then to others, which caused tribal warfare to simmer uneasily throughout the remainder of the year and well on into 1960. This intriguing caused a deputation of tribal sheikhs to travel to Baghdad to see Kassem to ask him to stop making trouble between them, to remove all Kurdish officials in Kurdish territory and to replace them with Arabs. Although the sheikhs stayed in Baghdad for three weeks, their requests were not met.

The Fifth Congress, of May 1960, had marked the beginning of the period of sharp deterioration of relations between Kassem and the Kurds, during which he pointedly refused to consider any form of Kurdish autonomy. Many DPK members were arrested and provincial branches closed down until by September only two remained open, that at Baghdad and that at Suleimaniya. Elsewhere DPK committee meetings were held in private houses with increasing secrecy. Kurds and Kurdish projects and schemes for improvement were ignored or neglected by the Iraqi Government. This attitude may have been partly caused because Kassem knew that many Kurdish politicians openly held Communist sympathies.

On the 3rd November 1960 Mullah Mustafa left for a visit to the Soviet Union, ostensibly to attend the October Revolution ceremonies, but actually to try to persuade the Russians to press the Iraqi Government to make concessions to the Kurds. Mullah Mustafa had perhaps been encouraged to do this by the tone of recent Soviet broadcasts, which were hostile to Kassem, but he failed in his mission and returned to Baghdad on the 13th January 1961, a disillusioned and bitter man. It was obvious to him that the Kurds would gain nothing from Kassem and little more from the Soviet Union, and that it was up to the Kurds themselves to do something about it if they wanted autonomy.

While Mullah Mustafa was away in the Soviet Union, tribal fighting broke out, although it was mid-winter, between the Barzanis and their traditional enemies, the Zibaris and the Baradostis. There had been vague surprise that Kassem had allowed Mullah Mustafa to visit the Soviet Union in the first place, but when tribal fighting erupted many inferred that Kassem, knowing this might happen as he had supplied the Zibaris and Baradostis with arms, wanted the Barzanis to be defeated and weakened.

In February 1961 a tribal clash occurred between the Barzanis and the Shaklawa tribe, in which its sheikh, Sadik Niran Osman, a landowner and ex-Member of Parliament, and a Kassemite Kurd, was killed. The murderers were reputed to belong to the DPK, and on the 9th March Ibrahim Ahmed, the Secretary of the DPK, was accused of his murder, but later the warrant for his arrest was withdrawn. This caused Ibrahim Ahmed to go underground, but he remained in Baghdad. On the 20th February Kassem cancelled a conference of Kurdish teachers, and on the 22nd March he closed down the newspaper, *Khabat*, the last remaining Kurdish paper in circulation. The increasingly hostile Arab attitude towards the Kurds in the capital made it necessary for Mullah Mustafa to maintain a private body-guard, and for the DPK building to have Kurdish guards to protect it from damage.

Relations between the DPK and the tribes, never good, took a turn for the worse in February 1961 when the Arkou tribe, based on Raniya, was preparing to revolt against the Government and asked for DPK aid, which did not materialize. The Arkou revolt turned out to be a damp squib, and recriminations followed; the Arkou alleged that the DPK had badly let it down, while the DPK insisted that it had given no promises to the Arkou and that it was still committed to employing only legal means in working for Kurdish autonomy.

In March 1961 Mullah Mustafa was allowed to leave Baghdad and return to Barzan, where he became the active, dominant Kurdish nationalist leader in the mountain setting. Although he remained the nominal Chairman of the DPK, he had little control or influence with that party, most of it resting in the hands of the five-man Politburo, especially with Ibrahim Ahmed, the Secretary. Critical as it was of Mullah Mustafa, the DPK continued to support him as the Kurdish national leader. Thus Mullah Mustafa had it both ways: he had a strong stake in tribal matters, through his leadership of the virile Barzanis, and a prestige position as head of the DPK. The DPK had practically no support at all in the mountains, and so was very reluctantly compelled to remain on good terms with its Chairman.

In June 1961 both Mullah Mustafa and the DKP presented petitions to Kassem asking for free use of the Kurdish language, for Kurdish schools, for a share in oil revenues from the Mosul and Kirkuk oilfields, and making other familiar Kurdish demands. These were examined by the Iraq Revolutionary Council and rejected. The DPK then presented another petition demanding a more favourable answer, but received no reply. Arab workers demonstrated outside the DPK headquarters in Baghdad, and in the scuffles Kurdish guards fired shots which killed and wounded several. Lokman, Mullah Mustafa's son, was placed under house arrest, as were other members of the DPK, while others went underground. Sheikh Ahmed Barzani, still friendly towards Kassem, was allowed to remain at liberty in Baghdad as a go-between between the Iraqi Government and Mullah Mustafa in the mountains. The DPK Politburo wanted to join Mullah Mustafa so as to batten on to his source of power, but he would not allow this, insisting that it stay underground in Baghdad to procure information and supplies.

4

THE REVOLT BEGINS

'There are three plagues in the world, the rat, the locust and the Kurd.'

Arab proverbs

The Kurdish Revolt began to gather momentum from March 1961, when Mullah Mustafa took to the mountains; it increased when the Barzanis were bombed by the Iraqi Air Force in September, and so were fully drawn into the struggle—which until then had been mainly inter-tribal—against the Kassem Government. The final die was cast in December of that year, when the DPK decided to give the revolt its full support, after which Mullah Mustafa and his followers and, to a far lesser extent, the DPK element, expanded to occupy large tracts of Kurdish territory in northern Iraq, consolidating their hold on them in 1962.

Traditional enmities die hard with the Kurds. When Mullah Mustafa rode into the mountains to take field command of his tribe, the Barzanis, his intention was to make it paramount and pay off a few old scores, and not really to rise in arms against the Kassem Government. However, deciding that the Barzanis were already far too powerful for his liking, Kassem stepped up his policy of bribing and arming tribes hostile to the Barzanis to fight them, and then followed about six months (the summer campaigning months) of inter-tribal fighting in the mountains. The main antagonists of Mullah Mustafa were the Zibaris and the Lolanis, and in the clashes and scuffles the Barzanis consistently came off best. Government troops were hardly involved in these hostilities. With some 5,000 fighting tribesmen—Barzanis, Kurdish and Assyrian allies—Mullah Mustafa attacked tribes that would not accept his domination, and seized strategic bridges and passes. Kassem replied by arming and bribing more tribes to fight against him. During this phase both the Barzanis and the Zibaris sought allies in the field. Mullah Mustafa found some in the several scattered pockets of surviving Assyrians, who had always resented control and indifferent treatment by the

74

Iraqi Arab Government. Although generally hostile to all Kurds, the Assyrians fought well for Mullah Mustafa, but the Zibaris hit back at them hard and on one occasion occupied Amadiya, an Assyrian town, and burnt the church. The Barzanis were victorious; burning crops and destroying villages as they advanced with their Assyrian and other allies, they pushed large numbers of Zibaris over the frontier into Turkey.

Despite these widespread disorders, almost amounting to anarchy, which the Government could not control, neither Mullah Mustafa nor Kassem wanted a direct and open confrontation with each other. But this was not the case with the Arkou, a tribe that had allied itself with the Barzanis. In the inter-tribal fighting the Arkou had been able to dominate most of the territory between Raniya, their traditional base, and Arbil to the north, reaching to link up with the Barzanis. The Arkou had become over-confident and aggressive, developing a contemptuous attitude towards the passiveness of the Government troops. On the 11th September 1961 a group of Arkou tribesmen, under Sheikh Abbas Mohammed, who was incensed by Kassem's policy of land reform, attacked an army column near Bazyan, on the route between Kirkuk and Suleimaniya, causing casualties.[1] On the 16th the Government responded by bombing Barzan, although the Barzanis had not taken any part in this ambush action. In fact, apart from a few isolated cases over which Mullah Mustafa had no control, neither the Barzanis nor their allies made any deliberate attack on the Iraqi Army. This incident at Bazyan swung the scales for Mullah Mustafa, who now came out openly against Kassem and his forces; and so somewhat reluctantly he and his Barzanis were drawn into the Kurdish Revolt to become its mainspring. But there was more to it than just that; it was a case of mutual fear and mistrust. Certain units of the 2nd Infantry Division, responsible for this part of Iraq, were being redeployed, although at this stage no extra reinforcements had actually been drafted into the region, and this was interpreted by Mullah Mustafa as a prelude to an attack on him in force by the Iraqi Army. On the other hand, this redeployment was being made because Kassem thought Mullah Mustafa and his armed tribesmen were about to sweep down on to the plains, probably to attack Kirkuk and Suleimaniya. Neither had wanted an open fight, and both had hesitated as long as they could, but in the tense war of nerves Kassem was the first to give way.

[1] It was reported that some 23 Government soldiers were killed.

Mullah Mustafa and his allies reacted swiftly and savagely, attacking police and border posts, driving out the personnel and taking possession, and also forcing their way into some towns and larger villages where there were no Government garrisons, such as Zakho. Army, police and frontier patrols were ambushed and blocks placed on all roads and tracks. The pressure against tribes on the Government side was kept up concurrently, with the result that within about a fortnight the Kurdish rebels dominated an area of territory stretching from Zakho, in the west, to nearly as far as Suleimaniya in the east, that included some 200 miles of Turkish and Persian frontier. When Kassem realized what was happening he ordered his 2nd Infantry Division to move into Kurdish rebel territory. As Iraqi soldiers advanced villages were shelled and destroyed, while aircraft dropped bombs, fired rockets and spewed bullets indiscriminately at targets on the ground. The Barzanis had no real friends, and the Government was able to bribe and persuade many of their temporary allies to turn against them. Zakho was reoccupied, as were other towns and villages, the Kurdish rebels evacuating with scarcely any resistance. This army offensive was superimposed on the concurrent inter-tribal fighting, but although the main roads were reopened, the Iraqi Army failed to impose its control over the countryside between them. Some attempts were made to do this, but they were feeble and soon subsided. In this Government September offensive aerial activity caused rebel tribesmen to disperse from their villages into the shelter of caves and rocky valleys. In these actions a number of casualties were incurred on both sides, but reliable figures were unobtainable. Almost at once casualties became a serious problem to the rebels as there was nearly a complete lack of doctors and medical facilities in Kurdish rebel territory.

It was not until the 24th September that Kassem admitted that a Kurdish tribal revolt had broken out and spread to one-third of Iraq, and that the rebels had burnt at least fifty villages. He boasted that the revolt had been put down, except for a few remnants which would be destroyed within a day or so, that Zakho had been reoccupied and that many tribesmen had fled over the border into Turkey. Kassem also alleged that Britain and America were responsible for this Kurdish revolt, that they had supplied the arms, that British subversive 'cells' had been discovered in Iraq, and that the British Embassy in Baghdad had spent £400,000 instigating the revolt. The following day Britain formally denied the allegations.

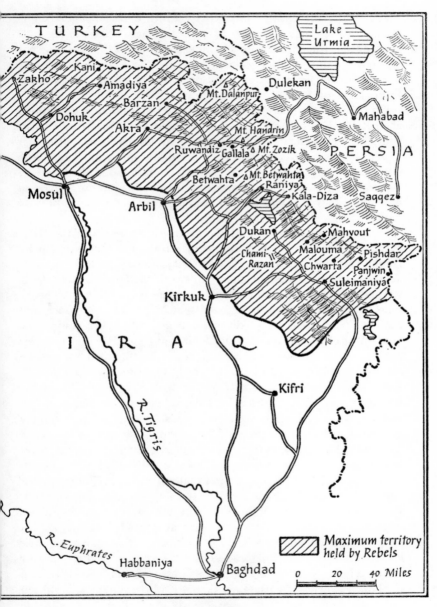

Northern Iraq

These wildly inaccurate statements set the tone for many communiqués that were to be issued by both sides in the months and years ahead, when false claims became the order of the day. Kassem also pointed out with heavy significance that the Kurdish Revolt had coincided with British troop movements to the south in relation to Iraqi claims on Kuwait.

On the 10th October Kassem announced that military operations against the Kurdish rebels had ended and that the Army was in complete control again. But this was by no means correct, although a large number of Kurds had been killed and many more rendered homeless through destruction caused by aircraft and artillery action. Accurate figures remained impossible to obtain, but some reports mentioned that '270 villages had been destroyed' and 'several towns damaged'.

During the summer of 1961 the Central Committee of the DPK became divided on the best course of action. The majority, led by Ibrahim Ahmed, the Secretary, wanted open war with Kassem to be delayed as long as possible, mainly to enable the DPK to build up its strength—it possessed few arms at this stage. He felt that open hostilities might attract army loyalty and sympathy back to Kassem, and that the DPK itself might disintegrate under full war strain. The vital lessons from the unfortunate Mahabad Republic influenced this faction, which were that neither the mountain tribesmen nor outside support could be relied upon. If it was to dominate the Revolt the DPK had to be prepared to fend for itself. The minority on the Central Committee, led by Jalal Talabani and Omar Mustafa, had been in favour of anticipating Kassem's expected attack, on the grounds that Kassem could not count upon the support or loyalty of the Army as he had so completely alienated it and lost its confidence; in any case, the armed forces were some one-third Kurdish in composition, albeit with a largely detribalized element. Both factions agreed that Jalal Talabani should travel into the mountains to consult Mullah Mustafa, still the nominal Chairman of the DPK, to see what his view was; the DPK still desperately needed to draw on his support and influence to impose itself upon the Kurds as their leadership in revolt. Mullah Mustafa's advice had been to wait for the time being and not to take any aggressive action unless Kassem used open violence against either the DPK or the Barzanis, or indeed any of their principal allies, particularly the Arkou. However, the decision was precipitated, as on the 23rd September 1961, at a press conference, Kassem declared the DPK to be dissolved, on the technicality of not having held an annual conference as was required under his Association Law. Two days later the Central Committee of the DPK decided to join openly in the Kurdish armed struggle against Kassem but, reluctant to leave Baghdad, it took no positive steps for some months, and in fact it was not until the first weeks of 1962 that a DPK armed force began to establish itself in the field.

In December the Central Committee finally realized that it could do no good by remaining in Baghdad, where it was hamstrung, on the pretence of negotiating with Kassem, who by this time had turned rigidly against the Kurdish cause. With extreme reluctance it left for the mountains. It knew that the mountains were dominated by Mullah Mustafa, and that by leaving the capital it would lose most of its direct contact with the outside world, but it also fully appreciated that if Mullah Mustafa were defeated, or came to terms with Kassem, without its knowledge or consent, the DPK would be doomed. Thus it was a case of sheer survival, but even so the Central Committee dragged its feet. Not until March 1962 did the DPK become effective in the southern part of Kurdish territory, in parts of the mountainous regions between Raniya and Suleimaniya, in a sector just south of Arkou country. Mullah Mustafa and his allied sheikhs would not tolerate the DPK in their areas.

In these deliberations Ibrahim Ahmed had compromised. He was a Communist who concealed his political views for practical purposes, as he wanted to win the co-operation of the mountain sheikhs, who suspected and disliked Communist aims. Also, he knew that if the DPK merged into the ICP it would lose its separate character and identity, and so forfeit the support of the Kurds, which it had largely enjoyed on Kurdish matters. Ibrahim Ahmed knew that if this happened Mullah Mustafa would be left the undisputed leader of the Kurds, whereas as long as he was nominally the Chairman of the DPK and maintained contact with it, he was potentially susceptible to its influence, the Politburo of the DPK considering that it held the real political power. The ICP had wanted to organize an Arab-Kurdish Front against Kassem on the grounds that his overthrow was the paramount aim and that Kurdish aspirations should take second place.

Abroad there was a great deal of indifference towards the Kurdish demand and spasmodic interest was only shown when it was thought it might serve some selfish national purpose. During the period of the union of Egypt and Syria (1958–61), President Nasser had consistently refused to recognize the Syrian Kurds as a cultural minority and had severely repressed any symptoms of nationalist tendencies, but later, after the dissolution of this union, and during his period of enmity with the Syrian Government, Radio Cairo supported the Kurdish national cause, as did Radio Damascus at times. On the 16th November 1961 the Central Committee of the DPK sent a message to U Thant, the UN Secretary General, accusing the Iraqi Army of genocide and asking for an international commission to investigate on the spot, but it received only the vaguest of replies.

By no means all Kurds in Iraq were dedicated to Kurdish nationalism. While many were passive, neutral or indifferent, more than a few actively supported Kassem against the Kurdish tribesmen and revolutionaries. Many senior Kurdish Army officers, Government officials and professional men, all well detribalized, having become Iraqi nationalists or at least believers in Iraqi national unity, were out of sympathy with the mountain Kurds. For example, there were usually two or three Kurdish ministers in most of Kassem's cabinets, and one of the three members of the select Sovereignty Council was always a Kurd. Deeply concerned as he was about the Army's loyalty to him, Kassem was worried whether, with its large element—about 30 per cent—of Kurdish soldiers, it could be relied upon to go into action against the mountain Kurds. In the opening stages of the Revolt he had not needed to worry so much, as the Kurds themselves were hopelessly divided in their hates and loyalties, and numerous Kurdish soldiers had become detribalized and urbanized; many were some two or three generations removed from their mountain forebears. The Barzanis, the mainspring of the Revolt, had few friends, and the national character of the Kurdish insurrection was not yet sufficiently obvious to attract wider Kurdish support. Kurds, in fact, predominated in the Kirkuk-based 2nd Infantry Division that garrisoned the northern provinces, and although from the beginning there was a deserter problem and instances of individual Kurdish soldiers and groups refusing to go on operations against the Kurdish rebels, the majority had marched against their compatriots quite cheerfully. About one-third of the officers in the Iraqi Army were Kurds, but they were spread more evenly throughout Iraq, and were generally more detribalized than their soldiers.

Normally fighting was suspended in the northern mountains of

Iraq between November, when snow blocked the passes, and the spring thaw, but Kassem ordered operations to continue without stopping through the winter—an order the Iraqi Army was completely incapable of carrying out. It was in no fit state to fight on throughout the bad weather; on the contrary, it had to withdraw a number of small outposts and garrisons as it was unable to supply them. On the other side, Mullah Mustafa and his allies continued to harass Government forces and unfriendly tribes for a couple of weeks longer, and so were able to reoccupy and consolidate their hold on large tracts of mountainous regions between Zakho and the Persian border. The Assyrian town of Amadiya was reoccupied and, despite Assyrian protests, a Kurdistan administration took over. Mullah Mustafa had little time for his temporary Assyrian allies. But by mid-December the weather was even too severe for Mullah Mustafa's followers, and they also slowed down to a halt, remaining passive until the early spring. On the 31st December 1961 Kassem admitted that the 'rebels' had taken advantage of heavy snowfalls and the withdrawal of some army units to 'renew their criminal acts'.

Mullah Mustafa launched his spring offensive in late March 1962 with some success, as Government troops were not geared to expect it so soon; snow still hampered normal communications and bad weather restricted Iraqi air activity. His partisans assaulted Iraqi garrisons at both Zakho and Dohuk. Reports indicated that over fifty Iraqi soldiers were killed in these two actions and over 150 wounded, but both garrisons remained in Government hands. Guerrilla activity was recommenced against military communications, while the main weight of Mullah Mustafa's armed followers was turned against tribes hostile to him. Within a fortnight several of them had been forced to take refuge over the borders in Turkey and Persia. Mullah Mustafa claimed (very over-optimistically) that in his spring offensive his Kurds inflicted more than 3,000 casualties on the Iraqi forces and their tribal allies.

During March 1962 Kassem had offered the Kurds a general amnesty if they would lay down their arms, but there had been no response or reply while the spring offensive was under way. It was not until the 20th April that Mullah Mustafa replied that he would cease fire only if the Kurds were granted autonomy within the Iraqi Constitution that guaranteed their legitimate political, social and cultural rights, and then only if the Kassem Government was replaced by a democratic one. At the same time Mullah Mustafa

F 81

issued a manifesto emphasizing that his aim was Kurdish autonomy within Iraq, and not Kurdish independence. This attracted some Arab sympathy and avoided alienating general Arab opinion. It had a result a few days later when a statement signed by several prominent Iraqi Arab leaders, supporting Mullah Mustafa's demands, was published in a Baghdad newspaper. Mullah Mustafa's manifesto was also supported by the ICP.

In the second quarter of 1962 neither side attempted any bold strategic or tactical moves against the other. The Government troops were seemingly content to remain on the defensive, securely entrenched in their camps, barracks or towns, merely occasionally essaying out on minor punitive raids and keeping the main communication roads open. The Army did not attempt to put into operation any serious scorched earth tactics or undertake any deliberate annihilation policy, although there was continual aerial activity, which caused Kurdish casualties. Most of the skirmishing was between the Government Auxiliaries, tribes hostile to Mullah Mustafa and his allies, and the Barzanis and their allies. On their part, Mullah Mustafa and his followers made no attempt to assault towns or garrisons held by Government troops, but concentrated instead upon disrupting army communications by blocking defiles, blowing up bridges and ambushing convoys and supply columns. The object was to demoralize the army garrisons by harassment and starvation, and on several occasions supplies had to be dropped by parachute to beleaguered army units, some of which fell wide of the mark and were seized by the Kurds. By using these tactics Mullah Mustafa claimed that in the three months from April to June 1962 he inflicted over 1,000 casualties on Government forces—but again this must be an exaggeration, and in their turn the Government forces, aided by the Air Force, inflicted many casualties on hostile Kurds. Mullah Mustafa did not scruple to use scorched-earth tactics as he worked ruthlessly to consolidate his hold over the territory between Zakho and the Persian frontier. He moved with what forces he could muster against those tribes that would not ally themselves with him, burning their crops, killing livestock and destroying villages, as he drove the inhabitants either over the borders into Turkey or Persia or down on to the plains to the south. In this manner Mullah Mustafa soon dominated most of the smaller tribes in his area (which, if they could, adopted a policy of expediency, and joined with the Barzanis, who were daily growing in strength and power), but soon he came abruptly up against more formidable foes, such as the Zibaris, Baradostis, Surchis and Herkis, living mainly to the south of Barzan, who had been supplied with money, arms and ammunition by Kassem to fight him. The wave of Kurdish nationalism that later attracted many Kurds to Mullah Mustafa's banner was as yet of marginal significance.

Kurdish tribesmen who had been pushed over the Persian border in Mullah Mustafa's spring offensive were later allowed to return to Iraq through mediation by the Shah, but the condition was made that Kassem should not enlist them to fight against the Barzanis again. Mullah Mustafa promised not to make them fight on his side against Government forces. Relations between the Persian and Iraqi Governments were seldom good, and at times were bad; this was typical of several behind-the-scenes contacts the Persian authorities had with Mullah Mustafa, for their own devious purposes to the annoyance of the Kassem régime. The Persian Government secretly poked its finger into the pie, sometimes to placate its own Kurdish border tribes, which were hostile to Mullah Mustafa and his Barzanis.

Although Mullah Mustafa was personally disliked and distrusted by most tribal sheikhs, who regarded him as a radical and deeply suspected the intentions of his Sovietized followers as much as they feared the aggressive Barzanis, nevertheless he became the natural and undisputed leader of Kurdish nationalism who, in 1962, symbolized the gradual overcoming of the Kurds' traditional inability to unite. He achieved this partly because of his former revolutionary activities in Barzani revolts and during the Mahabad Republic, partly because of his fighting Barzanis and partly because of his strong personality, but mainly perhaps because there was no other Kurdish leader of any reputation and stature available. Although relations between Mullah Mustafa and the Central Committee of the DPK were poor and steadily deteriorating,[1] it also accepted him as the national Kurdish leader and field commander, but with deep private reservations, as did so many others not committed to support the Government. Mullah Mustafa maintained a strictly independent attitude towards the ICP and all Iraqi Communists, although they openly spoke out in favour of his April Manifesto.

At first, apart from his personal bodyguard, which seemed to vary

[1] It was widely rumoured that late in 1962 Mullah Mustafa dismissed Ibrahim Ahmed from his position as Secretary of the DPK, but this was without foundation. David Adamson in *The Kurdish War*.

from about 50 to 100 men, Mullah Mustafa had to rely upon tribal irregulars or tribal militia to do the fighting for him. These tribesmen, or partisans, were either volunteers or, frequently, they were detailed by their sheikhs for this role, and were largely undisciplined and un-reliable—the Barzanis being somewhat less so while their allies were more so. As the Kurdish rebels did not hold a rigid front line, or even definite sectors of country, but merely seeped in and around Government posts and communications, the partisans were suitable for laying ambushes and making hit-and-run assaults. Especially were they of value in the preliminary inter-tribal clashes when Mullah Mustafa was striving to establish his dominance over stretches and tribes of the northern mountains. The partisans usually assembled for a particular action or raid, after which they returned to their homes to carry on their normal way of life, often hiding their weapons in caves or fields to avoid being disarmed by Government searches. Their disadvantages were that they would not move far from home, or stay in hostile territory too long, or agree to fight a particular enemy. They were fickle in that they might decide to stop or start fighting as the mood took them; they were completely unorganized, but as more Kurdish regular officers deserted from the Iraqi Army to join Mullah Mustafa, some were set to work to bring a semblance of order and regularity into the partisan movement. Tribesmen were still called out for the duration of a particular operation, usually lasting for two or three days only, but as additional numbers of them became available and willing, some were assembled and kept 'mobilized' for a period (which came to mean about a month), mainly to hold territory, guard strategic points and be available for instant use if either Government forces attacked or an opportunity presented itself. This system of part-time service developed gradually until there were always between 5,000 and 8,000 mobilized partisans under Mullah Mustafa's direct influence, but not always under his complete control. Previous Kurdish revolts had always been weakened by tribal differences and the fact there was no standing armed force to consolidate and hold gains. Mullah Mustafa was succeeding in over-coming both disadvantages by uniting a broader section (albeit by force and threats) of Kurds than ever before, and as the growing national flavour of the revolt attracted more Kurdish Army officers, who were able to train, organize and administer, he was able to build a standing army. During the summer and autumn of 1962 Mullah Mustafa claimed that he could muster up to 20,000 partisan tribesmen for an operation. Although this was a gross exaggeration, about half that number could have been made available.

Despite the partisans' successes, they remained mercurial and unreliable, so the need for a regular, disciplined armed force became even more obvious—a fact that was emphasized by the DPK Central Committee, which felt that if such a body was formed they would be able to gain control of it and so lessen dependence upon Mullah Mustafa's wild partisan tribesmen. Mullah Mustafa was reluctant to form an organized army, being satisfied with his partisan organization, which was improving and developing. It was the DPK in its sector of the mountains that first raised a standing force that remained fully mobilized, and which became known as the Pesh Merga. Mullah Mustafa reluctantly followed suit, although for over a year there was a very narrow distinction between his partisans and his Pesh Merga. As more officers and soldiers deserted from the Iraqi Army to join the rebels the Pesh Merga developed and swelled during the summer, and some sources estimate that by September 1962 it may have amounted to some 15,000 armed men, who had some semblance of military organization and discipline, but this figure must have included many partisans, so the true total might be nearer 5,000, most of whom were under Mullah Mustafa's direct control. Thus, in theory if not in practice, with the Pesh Merga, partisans and tribal warriors, Mullah Mustafa could field some 40,000 armed men, a formidable force, nearly half as large as the Iraqi Army—but there was of course far more to it than that.

This standing force, which was forged mainly in the DPK territory, was formally known as the Lashgar-i-Shoreshi-ye-Kurd, meaning the Kurdish Revolutionary Army. The leaders (at this stage there were no formal ranks) were known as Sar Merga, meaning 'leading death', and the soldiers as Pesh Merga, meaning 'facing death', the whole organization gradually became generally known as the Pesh Merga. At first it was largely tribal in composition, but contained a number of Kurdish regular army deserters,[1] which gave it a semblance of discipline and organization. To it were added over the months a sprinkling of urbanized Kurds who included a few lawyers and teachers (but no doctors), which formed a political element as the germ of Kurdish nationalism grew. The Pesh Merga was poorly supported at first and had many teething troubles. The mountain Kurds were reluctant to accept organization and discipline, and the tribal

[1] Estimated at 3,000 in the summer of 1962.

sheikhs were wary and suspicious that their authority was being sub-
verted, but gradually ex-Iraqi regular officers managed to weld it into
a rough mountain army, that in the DPK sector being more politically
inclined and motivated than the elements under Mullah Mustafa's
command.

The Pesh Merga was formed into small groups of just a few
fighters, known as 'dasteh' (platoons), which were, or could be,
merged to form a larger one known as 'pel' (companies), which
could in turn be grouped into a larger formation for operational purposes known as 'sar pel' (battalions), which usually had between 200
and 250 men. The organization of the Pesh Merga was extremely
sketchy and units and sub-units were known by the names of their
leaders. There were no formal headquarters at any level, not even the
highest, as Mullah Mustafa constantly moved from place to place, it
being alleged that he had the idea that if he did not Iraqi aircraft
would eventually locate him with the intention of killing him and his
bodyguard. However, in the DPK sector headquarters were set up
quickly and were functioning by the end of 1962.

For many months the Pesh Merga had no uniforms, although
special badges were early adopted, but from the autumn items of
military uniform, captured and purchased, were worn as they were
obtained. Apart from arms, the Pesh Merga had no military equipment of any sort, except a few captured radios, which were of little
use for inter-communication, owing to distances and blocking
mountain ranges, but were used to intercept Iraqi Army messages.
For a long while the supply service was poor, food being taken to
small outposts by donkey, or even manhandled. Later, a few battered
motor vehicles were acquired, but no trucks suitable for carrying
supplies along mountain roads.

Despite allegations and rumours to the contrary, neither the Soviet
Union nor the Western Powers provided the Kurdish rebels with any
aid or arms, and for many, many months their heaviest weapons were
50 mm. mortars. Mullah Mustafa continually said that his greatest
drawback was lack of artillery with which to bombard army camps
and towns from a distance. Arms were purchased on the black
markets, particularly in Beirut; the money was raised by Kurdish
agents in Lebanon, Persia, Syria and other countries and also, more
discreetly, underground in Iraq. The mountain Kurds who initiated
the Revolt, armed with old Mausers and French rifles, acquired the
majority of their weapons by capturing them from Government

forces, obtaining them by bribery, threats or tricks, and by their being brought over by army deserters. The Pesh Merga weapons were mainly small arms, mortars, bazookas, grenades and light machine-guns of mixed British, Soviet, Turkish and Persian origins. Ammunition was always an acute problem. Although Kurds usually handled rifles from boyhood, their sense of fire discipline was poor, and the overwhelming evidence seems to be that they were not good marksmen although, of course, there were exceptions to this generalization. Mortar bombs, for example, were in short supply and also had to be carried slowly and painfully through mountainous terrain to rebel positions, and so such mortars as were possessed by the Kurds were frequently impotent for lack of ammunition.

When the DPK Central Committee moved out from Baghdad into the mountains, Mullah Mustafa refused to allow it or the Politburo to enter the large stretch of northern terrain he was dominating. He sent out his partisans to ensure that this edict was enforced, so it was compelled to settle in an area to the south where Mullah Mustafa's writ did not run—roughly the mountains encompassed by the triangle Mount Sarband in the north, Suleimaniya in the south and almost to Kirkuk in the west. Thus Kurdish rebel territory was divided into two sectors, the northern one controlled by Mullah Mustafa, and the southern and very much smaller one by the DPK. In the DPK sector there were four main headquarters. One was near Malouma, near the Persian border in the centre of the triangle, which was commanded by Ibrahim Ahmed, the Secretary of the DPK. One was at Chwarta, some 30 miles to the north-west of Panjwin. Another was at Chami-Razan, just to the north of the Suleimaniya to Kirkuk road, which was commanded by Jelal Talabani, who showed a flair for military organization and became for a while the *de facto* DPK field commander. The other was at Betwahta, 20 miles north-west of Raniya, which was commanded by Omar Mustafa, this last being the northern-most point of the DPK sector, beyond which Mullah Mustafa's influence was too strong for the DPK.

The DPK had only about 650 rifles initially, but Jelal Talabani organized his Pesh Merga more effectively and quickly than Mullah Mustafa, indoctrinating as well as training and disciplining them. The DPK set about winning over the tribal sheikhs, and had some successes, as a few were persuaded to join the Party and others became interested in its aim, which was carefully disguised and altered for sheikhly consumption. At first, especially when numbers were small, the Pesh Merga was almost self-sufficient. As numbers increased a tax of 10 per cent was levied on the villagers and tribesmen, payable in cash or kind, to enable the rebel administration, Pesh Merga and partisans to function and exist. This tax, which was very unpopular as the people in the mountains themselves were poor and resented giving part of what little they had to a body that was better fed and cared for than themselves, was enforced in the DPK sector, but less efficiently by Mullah Mustafa in his areas.

Opposing the Kurdish rebels was the Iraqi Army, still in a far from healthy state after its frequent purges by Kassem and its internal dissensions, political and racial. At first it had fully supported him, as he had raised its pay in November 1958 and again in January 1959, by which time its conditions were very favourable compared with other professions and jobs in Iraq. The initial removal of literally all senior officers (all above the rank of brigadier), and subsequently of many others holding key appointments, as Kassem became suspicious of the Army's loyalty to him and apprehensive of its potential political power, had left it weak and inert. It was not surprising that it did not take bold, decisive action against the Kurdish rebels; indeed, such was the state of its morale and fitness for battle that it was to its credit that it maintained its positions in the mountains as it did throughout the winter and spring of 1962. Its arms were basically still those received sparingly from Britain, supplemented since 1958 by small quantities of Soviet material. Kassem did not want the Army to become too strong and independent, and was content with the existing Arab-Kurd-Christian schisms within it. He distrusted the Kurdish soldiers, but accepted them as a counter-balance to the Arab majority. He was faced with the huge deserter problem of Kurdish soldiers absenting themselves and taking their arms with them, which was extremely bad for morale. He had the additional morale-worrying problem of Kurdish soldiers refusing to fight Kurds, which was becoming contagious as the flame of Kurdish nationalism spread. Another reason why operations were not mounted against the rebels was the practical one that, as Kassem did not trust his Army very far, formations and units were issued with only two days' rations at a time and extremely limited supplies of ammunition.

The 2nd Infantry Division, having its headquarters and one brigade at Kirkuk, with a brigade at Mosul, another at Arbil, and another at Musayib, was gradually reinforced, from the spring of

1962, with other brigades. Apart from the few months in the summer when Kassem, alarmed by hostility generated by his claim to Kuwait, had to move troops southward in that direction, this build-up continued steadily until by the end of the year there were at least eight infantry brigades facing the Kurdish rebels. In July 1962 the headquarters of the 1st Infantry Division moved from Diwaniya in the south to Mosul, and assumed responsibility for what can be referred to as the Barzani sector, while the 2nd Infantry Division, still at Kirkuk, took on the smaller DPK sector. Some reports indicated that Kassem personally conducted the campaign in the field against the Kurdish rebels, but this was not so, and although he kept a firm grip on military policy and general strategy, operations were planned and conducted by recently promoted officers, who were comparatively youthful and inexperienced for such exacting executive posts and commands.

The main burden of war against the Kurds was carried by the Iraqi Air Force, which consisted of just under 300 aircraft disposed into six fighter squadrons (of Hawker Hunters, MiG–15s and MiG–17s), and one squadron of Ilyushin–28 bombers (it was in this sphere that most Soviet material had been received). Since September 1961 aircraft had continually strafed, machine-gunned, dropped napalm and fired rockets at Kurdish rebel villages and gatherings, driving many of the inhabitants to live in caves in the valleys. As the Kurds had neither aircraft, nor anti-aircraft weapons, this was a safe method to the Iraqis, and deadly effective as well. Aggressive aerial action shook Kurdish morale more than was admitted, and did much to unite the Kurds behind Mullah Mustafa and the DPK, and against Kassem and the Iraqi Government.

Air attacks were often unconnected with ground operations, and were deliberately designed to promote terror. Mullah Mustafa's staff alleged that in January 1962, 500 Kurdish villages had been attacked and some 80,000 people made homeless, and that in June 50,000 people had been killed by air attacks; other, more realistic claims indicated that some 3,000 had been killed and that 180,000 were homeless. Figures of wounded varied wildly. In July and August, in an all-out effort to demoralize and subdue the Kurds, aerial activity was intensified. The one exception and anomaly was the town of Barzan which, apart from the single, initial occasion, was immune from air attacks, because Sheikh Ahmed lived there, or went there frequently. The old sheikh had openly declared his loyalty to Kassem, and said that the Kurdish Revolt was a waste of Kurdish blood. Mullah Mustafa respected his brother's view, but did not agree with it. The real reason for the bombing immunity was probably that Sheikh Ahmed was a most useful and vital intermediary between Mullah Mustafa, and indeed the DPK, and Kassem.

The other forces engaged in fighting against the Kurdish rebels were the Government Auxiliaries, who came to be called the 'Jash' by their enemies. The word means 'little donkeys', a derisive expression. They were recruited from tribes traditionally hostile to the Barzanis, such as Zibaris and Baradostis, but there were others as well, including a number of Barzanis, anxious to keep in with Kassem and out of sympathy with their tribe and Mullah Mustafa. The Barzanis often squabbled amongst themselves. The Jash stayed in the field for set periods of time, depending upon Government pressure, persuasion and bribes, and at their maximum probably numbered over 10,000. Their strength dwindled as it became less popular to fight against Mullah Mustafa, campaigning became less rewarding and the fighting more dangerous. The Jash remained organized on a clan basis and received only general directions, rather than precise orders, from the Iraqi Army commanders they were supporting, and so did not develop any real military ability or discipline. They were employed to practise the age-old policy of scorched-earth in conjunction with regular army operations, to burn crops, kill livestock and demolish buildings, and generally keep the Kurdish rebels preoccupied, so as to give the Army a respite from pressures. They clashed frequently with the Barzanis and their allies, and in particular they operated against the Assyrians; several instances of atrocities occurred. Mullah Mustafa did not now favour scorched-earth tactics, perhaps because he realized that it would not be to his ultimate benefit to lay waste his own territory, which could barely feed his followers. There were exceptions to this ban, but chiefly when his tribesmen got out of hand. The activities of the Jash lessened as the months passed and their numbers decreased, until there only remained a hard core of some 5,000, who were gradually forced on the defensive.

Kurdish rebels dominated the northern mountains from the Syrian border to the edge of the Khanakin oilfield, a crescent of some 300 miles in length and up to 70 miles deep. Within this crescent, along those sections of the Turkish and Persian frontiers, Iraqi Government presence had disappeared, as the police and frontier guards had joined the rebels, and in the few villages where they were still in uniform they were openly collaborating with them. The situation throughout the summer of 1962 was that the Army controlled the main roads during daylight while the Kurds retained the freedom of the countryside. The main road from Arbil to Ruwandiz, for example, was almost continually blocked by sabotage. The aim of the Pesh Merga and partisans, operating in small groups armed with light machine-guns and light mortars, was to cut the roads in an attempt to starve garrisons and ambush convoys by day, a form of warfare that suited their character.

At night troops stayed defensively in their camps, thus allowing the Kurds freedom of movement, and even by day the Army only left its entrenched garrison when absolutely necessary, although the soldiers were able to use the main road, usually with immediate overhead cover. After dawn each morning Soviet T–34 tanks rumbled out from camps to break and clear any road blocks erected the previous night. Kurdish ambushes, road blocks and raids brought retaliation in the form of shelling and aerial activity. Environment played a part in this type of warfare, as the tribesmen were at home in the mountains while the Arabs from the plains were not, and even a large proportion of the Kurdish soldiers had been brought up away from mountainous terrain. In the north Kurdish officers were in the minority and so, despite a degree of training and discipline, the Iraqi Army facing the Kurdish rebels had an inferiority complex as regards mountain warfare.

In the early autumn the Kurds talked of spreading the war first to Arbil and then to Kirkuk (both of which they claimed to control at night) and afterwards to Suleimaniya, which they were able to operate in fairly freely despite the presence of the Army garrison, but nothing came of these visions and operations began to slow down. As the winter snows fell the partisans returned to their villages, and both Mullah Mustafa and the DPK had difficulty in holding together a small cadre of the newly formed Pesh Merga. Kurdish wars, usually fought for feud or gain, invariably ended when winter approached. On the Government side the momentum slowed down to a stop at about the same time, despite the occasional false news release proclaiming a brilliant victory. Some small garrisons were withdrawn and others became isolated, a few having to be supplied by air throughout the winter.

During the winter of 1962–3 small groups of Kurds entered the towns of Arbil, Kirkuk and Suleimaniya to kidnap those considered to be traitors to the Kurdish national cause, taking them away and shooting them; it was estimated that over fifty were eliminated in this manner in Suleimaniya alone. These urban underground terrorist activities caused some concern and had the effect of cooling down the opinions of those detribalized Kurds who were against the Revolt. To avoid causing unpleasant repercussions in the Soviet Union, and to some extent in Western countries, the ICP and Communists were left alone.

Prisoners were taken by both sides. The Arab–Iraqi ones seized by the Kurds were usually released after being disarmed, unless they were considered to be of some importance or use, as they did not want the burden of feeding and guarding them. A few were kept for labouring jobs and other duties round Pesh Merga camps. Kurdish soldiers taken prisoner by the Kurdish rebels were usually persuaded to turn their coats and join the Pesh Merga. If they did not they were made to work on roads. The Kurds invariably claimed that such personnel were not 'prisoners' but were 'deserters' from the Government forces. Any Jash captured had a rougher time and were kept to undertake labouring tasks. In November (1962) the Kurdish rebels claimed that they held about 2,000 prisoners, of whom half were Jash. The same month they claimed that only 172 Kurdish fighting men had been killed or wounded in battle, and that none had been taken prisoner—but these claims and figures were dubious. The Government forces had also taken a number of prisoners, and presumably held about the same number—probably on the hostage principle. Other smaller fry were released on giving a promise not to bear arms against the Government again.

Surprisingly enough in this partisan-type war, the vital oil pipeline running from Kirkuk, through Baiji and Haditha, to Abu Kamal and Baniyas in Syria, received little sabotage attention. Mullah Mustafa's view was that it would be foolish to disrupt a source of wealth of which the Kurds hoped eventually to obtain a generous share. Also, both Mullah Mustafa and the DPK held the view that to interfere with the oil pipeline would alienate Western and world opinion, although a DPK minority view differed. A few attempts were made, the first occurring on the 30th August 1962, when a small group of Kurds blew up part of the pipeline some seven miles from Kirkuk, but it hardly affected the flow of oil at all. There had previously been an assault on some oil installations in the Ain Zallah oilfields in

Turkey, near the Syrian border, in which some buildings were destroyed and some lives lost, but the Kurds responsible were extremists,
and this action was not authorized by either Mullah Mustafa or the
DPK. In a rather misguided effort to bring their case and circumstances to the attention of the West, on 10th October 1962 a British
oil technician was kidnapped by the Kurds and kept as a 'guest' for
some weeks before being released, and on the 26th November another British subject was seized and given similar treatment. At about
this time, too, a tiny handful of foreign journalists managed to penetrate Kurdish rebel territory and send back reports.[1] Although both
Mullah Mustafa and the DPK disclaimed any contact with Kurds in
adjacent countries, saying that their struggle was mainly against the
Kassem régime, they had obviously hoped that their actions would
have set off some train of discontent, and this did occur briefly in
Turkey, where, when a coalition government formed in 1961, a new
policy was adopted. The 1961 Turkish Parliamentary Constitution
that followed the Army coup brought about a proliferation of political parties, some of which were left-wing in bias, and this new 'wind
of political freedom' reached the Kurds as well. The 'Mountain
Turk' myth began to take a tumble as the various political parties
found willing listeners among the Kurds in eastern Anatolia. There
were demonstrations and speeches, but no Kurdish nationalist
movement emerged, mainly because the political agents fomenting
discord had no time for such views.

However, from 1962 the Turkish Government viewed Kassem's
régime with increasing disfavour, relations between the two countries deteriorated and there were a number of border incidents. Even
so, the Turkish Government did not want its Kurds to become involved in the Revolt, and did its best to prevent arms and supplies
being smuggled across its border to Mullah Mustafa. A 12-mile-wide
strip of territory, extending for the whole length of the joint Turkish–
Iraqi frontier, was evacuated of people and became a forbidden zone,
which was heavily garrisoned and well patrolled by Turkish soldiers.
These measures did much to restrict cross border traffic, but did not
completely prevent it.

On the 9th July 1962 an Iraqi aircraft bombed a Turkish frontier
post. On the 16th of the same month a similar incident occurred in
which two Turkish soldiers were killed. The Iraqi Government apolo-

---

[1] They included David Adamson, of the *Sunday Telegraph*, and Dana Adam
Schmidt, writing for the *New York Times*.

gized, claiming that the incidents were accidental, but the Turkish Government ordered fighter aircraft to patrol its frontier with Iraq. On the 16th August this patrol engaged and shot down an Iraqi aircraft, killing the pilot. On the 18th the Iraqi Government protested that the incident had occurred 48 miles inside Iraqi territory, and went on to allege that 'outlaws' in Turkey were helping to organize revolt in Iraq, either with Turkish connivance or because the Turkish Government could not control its frontiers. The Turks denied these allegations, and on the 23rd recalled their Ambassador from Baghdad. There was some liaison between the Kurds in Turkey and those in Iraq, but it was spasmodic, ineffectual and with hardly any influence on the course of the Revolt.

In Persia, where since May 1961 the Shah had closed the Majlis and ruled by decree, the situation was somewhat different, and there was no doubt considerable secret satisfaction at Kassem's many problems, especially the Kurdish Revolt. A Kurdish language station in Persia broadcast news of the Kurdish Revolt in Iraq as it could be obtained, and continued to do so right on until the summer of 1963, when the Persian Government, appreciating at last the international potential of the Iraqi insurrection, took a harder line towards it. The tribes on the Persian side of the Iraq border were those generally hostile to the Barzanis, and in particular they disliked Mullah Mustafa, remembering his harsh actions against them when escaping from Mahabad in 1946. Especially hostile was the 12,000-strong Mamash tribe, whose tribal territory covered sections of the frontier opposite Ruwandiz and Barzan, it being said that, when escaping out of Persia with his Barzanis in 1946 and 1947, Mullah Mustafa murdered eleven aghas (clan chiefs).[1] As the national character of the Revolt had not become obvious to the Persians, they were not unduly worried as they felt they had their own Kurds well under control, so while officially disclaiming any sympathy with the Iraqi Kurds, they in fact allowed a certain amount of arms, ammunition and supplies to be sent across the border to both Mullah Mustafa and the DPK— the latter, developing contacts in Persia, had the sympathy of the banned Communist Tudeh Party. While agents, liaison officers and couriers frequently crossed the frontier, large concentrations of troops were sent to the frontier regions in the mountains. Unofficial talks in Baghdad, in July 1962, between Sheikh Ahmed and Kassem came to

---

[1] According to David Adamson.

nothing, mainly because Kassem insisted on 'pardon and reconstruction' only, refusing to grant concessions to the Kurds at all. Secret contacts continued fruitlessly until the 10th January 1963, when Kassem again offered the Kurds amnesty if they surrendered within ten days; the period was extended to the end of that month, but the Kurds made no response.

The Iraqi Baathists had originally supported the coup that brought Kassem to power but since then they had progressively turned against him. The Baathist Party of Iraq shared with its Syrian counterpart the common aim of uniting Iraq and Syria, but it differed in its methods. The Iraqi Baathists were themselves also split on the attitude to be taken towards President Nasser's disapproval of Kassem. After the failure of the attempt on the life of Kassem in 1959, many were arrested and others fled the country, but although nominally illegal the Baathist Party was allowed to exist and was left much alone by the security police, perhaps because Kassem wanted it to counter balance other power-seeking factions. By June 1961 a new Central Committee had been formed. The Kassem amnesties enabled it to build up a strong underground political organization and a street militia that began to be powerful in the capital.

After the failure of the Baath-inspired riots and the activities of the Baath street militia to make any impression on the Kassem Government, the Central Committee concluded that power could only be obtained with Army help, and so it was decided to make contact with the Free Officers. By the end of 1961 a Joint Free Officers and Baathist organization had come into being (which later became the National Council of the Revolutionary Command, the NCRC). The officers this time were mainly from the Air Force. In March 1962, when Colonel Taher Yahya, the leading personality in the Free Officers movement, was dismissed from the Army by Kassem, he sought the support of the Kurds for his group and approached Ibrahim Ahmed, Secretary of the DPK. In subsequent talks Ibrahim Ahmed offered Kurdish support for the proposed coup against Kassem in return for Kurdish autonomy. This was not accepted immediately, and only after some months of hesitation did Colonel Taher Yahya verbally agree and ask the Kurds to nominate six potential ministers for the anticipated new government. There had been considerable initial difficulty in persuading the Baathists to agree to the Free Officers contacting the DPK, as they were extremely suspicious of it, feeling that it was almost Communist

95

in nature. They were reluctant to support Taher Yahya in bringing the Kurds into the plot, but they realized that they might have their uses and that Kurdish support would be valuable in consolidating the nation behind them once they had toppled Kassem. The DPK consulted Mullah Mustafa, who nominated Jelal Talabani, Omar Mustafa and four others who were not members of the DPK; Ibrahim Ahmed was not nominated, as he had hoped, but by this time he was well out of favour with Mullah Mustafa.

In January 1963 there was a meeting between the Baathists and the Kurds, at which the Baathist spokesman was Ali Salih al-Sadi and the Kurdish spokesman was Salem Abdullah Yousefi. It was afterwards claimed that at this meeting Sadi accepted the Kurdish claim for autonomy and that the term 'decentralization' was not even mentioned—but no written undertaking in this matter was given. The Baathists did not trust the Kurds, but simply wanted them to refrain from taking advantage of the armed forces to improve the rebel positions in the field, and not to attack, while they were effecting the coup against Kassem. The Baathists said they did not need active Kurdish help in the project, but that if they failed they wanted the conspirators to be given sanctuary in Kurdish rebel territory. In return for this the Kurds claimed that the Baathists and Free Officers promised Kurdish autonomy and four seats in the new Cabinet. The Baathists agreed to inform the Kurds in advance of the date of the coup so that they would be prepared, but as they did not trust them they deliberately failed to do so. The Kurds were as surprised as the rest of the people of Iraq when it occurred.

The Baathists became restless, especially as the suspicious Kassem began to put pressure on them immediately after the strike of Baathist students at the Baghdad University in December 1962 and the riots in January 1963 in which the Baathist militia, now once again openly on the streets of the capital, played such a prominent part. On the 4th February Kassem retired some fifty-eight Free Officers with Baathist sympathies, and he was planning other repressive measures against them.

After being postponed several times, the coup against Kassem was finally effected on the 8th February 1963 by a group of Free Officers, practically all from the Air Force, based on the Habbaniya airfield camp. The radio station in Baghdad was seized and aircraft bombed the Rashid Camp near Baghdad, where the Presidential Guard lived. The Baathist militia, prominent in green arm bands, took to the streets where for some hours it battled with the Communists, who did not want to see Kassem deposed. The Baathist militia won the day. Then, urged by Free Officers, it surged towards the Defence Ministry building, where Kassem and some 700 loyal troops were besieged. After a ten-hour battle, in which the building was shelled and bombed from the air, Kassem surrendered and was killed. During this tense period the bulk of the Army in Baghdad sat watchfully on the fence, but as it had no affection for Kassem it gradually rallied to the Free Officers when it saw what was happening. Kassem had just previously boasted that there had been thirty-eight attempts to kill him since he came to power.

The victorious junta, which called itself the National Council of the Revolutionary Command (the NCRC), appointed Colonel Abdul Salem Aref to be its President,[1] and the first Cabinet consisted mainly of Baathists of the non-Nasser type and Free Officers. The garrisons at Mosul and Kirkuk, after hesitation, came out in support of the NCRC, the only flash of real opposition being brief resistance by the Communists at Basra—Kassem had hardly any friends who were willing to fight for him. On the 15th February 1963 Colonel Abdul Salem Aref promoted himself Field-Marshal, the first in Iraq.[2]

After starting off so well Kassem progressively lost the support of influential sections of the community such as the Army, the Baathists and the Kurds, until the only people thinking well of him were the poorer classes,[3] who hoped he might alleviate their lot but who had no effective means to help him, and the Communists, who wanted him to remain in power a little longer to curb the Army and crush the Baathists, who were eclipsing them. The Kurdish war had made Kassem extremely unpopular in many quarters. The Army did not like the frustration of stalemate caused by tight curbs, the tax-payers did not like the continual high expenditure, and the actions of the Air Force were alienating many of the detribalized Kurds who were not at all in sympathy with the aims of the Revolt. Most saw the war as splitting, rather than uniting, Iraq, and there had been petitions by

[1] He, with other Baathists, had been released from detention by Kassem on the 25th November 1961.

[2] The only other Arab Field-Marshals at this time were Field-Marshal Amer, of Egypt, and Field-Marshal Sallal, of the Yemen.

[3] They were mainly peasants from southern Iraq, many of whom thronged the streets of Baghdad, causing riots and taking part in demonstrations in support of Kassem. They were called 'Sarifa' (shanty town) dwellers. In 1963, they were rounded up and transported back to their homes, their shanty towns on the outskirts of the capital being bulldozed away.

Arabs presented to Kassem, one as late as the 25th January 1963, urging him to negotiate with the Kurds. Kassem probably became a victim of his own propaganda, believing that he could not in the national interest give the Kurds autonomy, and so he had to continue with the war against them. As a shrewd soldier, however, he obviously knew that his Army, weak and listless as he had made it, could not win by military means. It was most probably true that he wanted the Kurdish war to continue at a low smouldering level to absorb the restless energy and ambitions of the politically minded officer corps, which he knew had turned against him. But again, Kassem might not have quite realized the magnitude of the military problem, feeling that he could easily contain it and perhaps later, in due course, crush it whenever it was expedient for him to do so. If this was the case, he was misled by his own information services and propaganda, which gave it out to the world that the Kurdish rebels were exhausted and that only small pockets still held out in the mountains—assertions that were far from true.

THE SECOND OFFENSIVE

'In need you get to know both your friends and your enemies.'

Kurdish proverb

Following the coup, both the Aref régime and its opponents sought Kurdish support, and the NCRC was quick off the mark when, on the 8th February 1963, it issued a communiqué appealing for the end 'of the glorious insurrection of the Kurds'. For their part, Mullah Mustafa and the Kurds generally welcomed Kassem's overthrow, and although in fact they had taken no part in the coup, they were anxious to claim some credit. Mullah Mustafa boasted that he could have advanced deep into the heart of Iraq with his Pesh Merga as the armed forces were so weak and disorganized, but he had not done so. He said he would cease operations and wait for the NCRC to implement its promises to the Kurds.

On the 12th February the Committee for the Defence of the Kurdish People's Rights issued a statement saying that any association between Kurds and Arabs must be based on an autonomous Kurdish government, the evacuation of Kurdish territory by Iraqi troops and an equitable division of state revenues, especially oil royalties, between Kurd and Arab. This was more extreme than anything Mullah Mustafa had demanded so far. A second statement, issued on the 15th, denied that the Kurdish movement had anything to do with Communism. This Committee was an international Kurdish one with independent views, having its headquarters at Lausanne, in Switzerland, which set itself up to represent Kurdish national interests abroad and to collect funds. It had some contact with Mullah Mustafa, and although it did not always see eye to eye with him, it supported him as the Kurdish national leader.

The cease-fire became effective immediately. Mullah Mustafa was reluctant to give open and full support to the Aref régime until it fulfilled Kurdish demands, but both he and the Politburo of the DPK were willing to enter into negotiations with the new Government, and Jalal Talabani was nominated to be the Kurdish negotiator. Talks between a Kurdish delegation, led by Talabani, and the Government began on the 19th February, but were adjourned two days later when Talabani left with an Iraqi Government party to visit Cairo for the celebration of the fifth anniversary of the formation of the United Arab Republic. While Talabani was in Cairo President Nasser assured him of his sympathy for Kurdish aspirations. Nasser was in favour of some concessions for the Kurds in Iraq, but not complete autonomy or secession. The USA had sent a message to Mullah Mustafa saying that it would support an autonomous Kurdistan, if one evolved from the negotiations.

Talks were resumed on the 25th, but when the Kurds asked that the verbal promises given by the NCRC be put in writing, the Government would not agree that it had made any. Negotiations, which had started so well, now began to falter, and difficulties arose over the term 'decentralization'. At a press conference on the 28th Talabani said that the Kurds had observed the cease-fire since the coup to give the new Government a chance, but he made it clear that while the Kurds would accept central control of the armed forces and foreign affairs, they demanded that all other matters pertaining to them should be handled by a Kurdish administration.

On the 1st March 1963 Talabani went north to consult Mullah Mustafa, who was then near Suleimaniya, and he was followed on the 4th by an Iraqi Government delegation that included two Kurdish ministers.[1] On the 9th the Government put forward proposals as a basis for discussion. The NCRC stated, on the 10th, that a compromise had been reached, and that it had agreed to grant the Kurds 'national rights' on the basis of 'decentralization'. The following day Ali Saleh Sadi, the Deputy Premier, said that the Kurds would remain attached to the central Government for foreign, economic and military affairs. Speaking for the Kurds, Salem Abdullah Yousefi replied that the Kurds would accept 'decentralization' and would be represented on a Government committee which was to be set up to work out details. Yousefi also complained that, although the Kurds had released all their prisoners, the Government had set free only 10 per cent of the Kurds they had captured or detained; he was not prepared to give way on that point. The Government reply was that many of the Kurdish prisoners had already been released, and that an amnesty would soon be announced.

Negotiations now became more difficult, and were complicated by

[1] Fuad Aref, Minister of State, and Baba Ali, Minister of Agriculture.

the proposed federation of Syria and Iraq, which would have meant that the Kurds would then become a minority of some 2 million in a population of some 13 million. After a break, negotiations were resumed in Baghdad towards the end of April, by which time the Kurdish demands had increased considerably. No longer were they content with equality with the Arabs in Iraq. They insisted on an autonomous Kurdistan, still within the Iraq constitution, which was to include the whole of the provinces of Arbil, Suleimaniya and Kirkuk, and the parts of the provinces of Mosul and Diyala where the Kurds were in the majority. The boundaries were deliberately vague, it being intended to include as many oilfields as possible. They demanded that one-third of all oil revenues be devoted to the Kurds, that there be a Kurdish Vice-President, that one-third of all seats in the Central Government go to Kurds, that the Deputy Chief of Staff be a Kurd, and that a number of other senior defence and governmental positions be held by Kurds. These demands took President Aref and his Arab ministers aback, and caused them to harden and change their attitude. The good intention to give some concessions vanished. Although negotiations continued, tension between the two sides rose, and President Aref simply played for time.

The Soviet Union was delighted when the Kurds made such heavy demands, and supported them openly. At this stage there was no real indication that the DPK was not pro-Communist, and so if Soviet influence could be gained with the Kurds, further inroads might be made towards the heart of the Middle East, thus causing anxiety to CENTO countries. The Aref Government responded by alleging that the Soviet Union was not only supporting the Kurds in a propaganda war, but was also supplying them with arms, which at this stage was very doubtful.[1] It also claimed that the USA, UAR, China and Israel were actively co-operating with and helping the Kurdish rebels. In May 1963, on Soviet instigation, the Mongolian People's Republic asked the UN to put the Kurdish question before the General Assembly, but this was later withdrawn in September. Opinion in Western countries tended to favour Kurdish aspirations, but as the CENTO forward defence line ran along the centre of the mountains in Kurdish territory, there was some anxiety in case a weak in-

---

[1] There is considerable doubt that the Soviet Union was giving any material aid to the Kurdish rebels, although Ghassemlou wrote, 'The Kurdish people received substantial help from socialist countries, particularly from their mighty neighbour, the Soviet Union.' *Kurdistan and the Kurds.*

dependent or autonomous Kurdistan might fall under Soviet domination, so none voiced any positive opinions.

At first President Aref tried to be friendly with President Nasser, but Nasser did not respond, and relations between them cooled when a Baathist coup in Syria caused a federation of Egypt, Syria and Iraq to be mooted. Aref had to contend with a strong trend of opinion in Iraq that the country should in some way be linked to Egypt, which was contrary to his own view. Accordingly, on the 11th May 1963, he formed a new Government which excluded Nasserites, and at the same time carried out a purge of pro-Nasser officers in the armed services. On the 25th May the Government announced that it had discovered a plot to arrest President Aref and members of the NCRC, to carry out massacres at certain Army camps, and to destroy the Baathist National Guard. The NCRC gave it out that 60 military officers and 120 civilians had been arrested. The National Guard had evolved from the former Baathist street militia, and boasted that it was over 40,000 strong. It was becoming active in major cities and towns.

Increased Kurdish demands caused the Aref Government to conclude that there was no option but to reopen the war. It was only prepared to give way on the language issue, but little else, while it seemed that Mullah Mustafa and the DPK were equally adamant. During the month of May additional troops were moved north from the region of Basra; as Iraq had practically abandoned its claim to Kuwait, it could accordingly afford to denude the south of military units. By the end of the month nearly three-quarters of the Army had been concentrated facing Kurdish territory, and was involved in guarding or blocking mountain routes, building or manning fortifications, or preparing for operations. From the 23rd May curfews and other restrictions were successively placed on 'mixed areas', and military establishments and oil installations were declared to be 'prohibited zones' where persons could be fired at without warning. Mullah Mustafa responded to these pressures by appealing to Kurds living in or near such places to return to their mountain homes, but few did so.

Jalal Talabani continued to lead the Kurdish delegation, and spent from the 16th May until the 3rd June in Egypt unsuccessfully trying to persuade President Nasser to use his influence to help the Kurds. When in Beirut on his way back to Iraq, he was warned that a Government military offensive against the Kurds was about to commence, so he left for Europe where he remained for a while. About the same time Mullah Mustafa had been given similar information, and he had appealed directly to Ahmed Hassan Bakr, the Premier, not to break off negotiations, in answer to which Bakr had blandly replied that the Iraqi troop movements had no offensive purpose.

The Aref Government had made up its mind. It issued an ultimatum accusing the Kurds of asking for impossible conditions, and promising pardons to deserters if they surrendered within three days. The time limit was extended but no Kurds came forward. On the 8th June a dawn-to-dusk curfew was imposed around the Habbaniya air camp, when curfew breakers could be shot on sight, while other restrictions were imposed in the Suleimaniya, Kirkuk, Arbil and Mosul military zones, all of which were placed under a single Military Governor, Brigadier Fathi Sakalli. In Baghdad, Saleh Mardi Ammash, the Defence Minister, handed new proposals to the Kurdish delegation, but the following day, when the delegation reached Kirkuk, its personnel were arrested.

On the 10th June the NCRC announced that it was beginning military operations against the Kurds, and ordering the rebels to cease all hostile activities and surrender their arms within 24 hours. It accused Mullah Mustafa of being an enemy of the revolution, harbouring Communists, attacking police posts and Army patrols, and raiding villages; it placed a reward of £100,000 on his head, dead or alive. The NCRC authorized Brigadier Sakalli to set up emergency courts empowered to impose death sentences on anyone aiding the rebels, and he said that any village that harboured or helped the rebels would be destroyed. The following day further Government decrees ordered all inhabitants of the northern provinces to surrender their arms immediately, imposed dawn-to-dusk curfews on the towns of Suleimaniya, Arbil and Kirkuk, and directed all Kurds who had settled on the outskirts of Kirkuk since 1958 to return to their homes. On the 20th the two Kurdish ministers in the Aref Government resigned, while a number of Kurdish officers and Government officials were suspended.

Abroad, the Lausanne-based Committee for the Defence of the Kurdish People's Rights announced, apparently without consulting either Mullah Mustafa himself or the DPK, that Mullah Mustafa had rejected the Iraqi Government ultimatum. Also on the 10th the Syrian Government stated that it would give all necessary aid to the Iraqi

Government to help crush the revolt. A Syrian brigade had already moved into western Iraq, ready to go into action if required. President Nasser remained silent for the time being, but as relations between the UAR and the Baathist régimes of Iraq and Syria became more strained, Radio Cairo began to voice strong criticism of the campaign that was being mounted against the Kurds.

During the cease-fire period the Kurdish rebels had not been idle. They had stocked up with food and obtained more arms, but ammunition remained a problem. It was estimated that they were able to put about 25,000 armed men in the field (slightly more than in the first offensive), of which some 15,000 were Pesh Merga scattered in small units, the remainder being partisans. Kurdish claims that their forces in the field and their reserves exceeded 100,000 were still considered to be far too high. The standard of organization and training of the Pesh Merga had improved slightly, but that of the partisans remained low and their idea of battle tactics primitive. Still in tribal groups, the partisans would not, for example, accept the conventional principle of covering fire and that when attacking they must all assault together, or not at all. Tribal sheikhs remained reluctant to relinquish any of their traditional authority.

The bulk of these rebel forces were in the north, in the Barzani sector, while on the Central and Eastern fronts (that is, in the DPK sector) there were only 650 Pesh Merga, but they were better disciplined, organized and controlled; indeed, they gave the Iraqi forces almost as much trouble as did those under Mullah Mustafa's command. Partisans were also organized and mustered in the DPK sector, but in proportionately fewer numbers. Mullah Mustafa still had no proper command headquarters from which to direct operations and he still moved continually from place to place, sometimes with an escort of as few as fifty armed men. He knew that the Iraqi Government wanted his death, and he feared that aircraft action might be directed against him personally. On the other hand, in the DPK sector battle headquarters had developed at Betwahta, Chami-Razan, Malouma, Mahvout[1] and Chwarta, which enabled more effective resistance.

On the early morning of the 10th June Government troops moved into action against the Kurds (although there had been skirmishing on the previous day) on three separate fronts, deploying the equivalent of four infantry brigades (that is, divisional strength) on each.

[1] Sometimes spelt Mawat.

The northern one was directed against the Barzani sector, commanded by Mullah Mustafa, the central one against the DPK forces commanded by Omar Mustafa, and the eastern one against the DPK forces directed from Chami-Razan. During the first week of this second offensive Government troops, consisting of some twelve infantry brigades, supported by artillery, armour and aircraft, slowly pushed their way forward into the mountains in this three-pronged advance, securing the lines of communication and picqueting the hills as they leap-frogged along.

On the northern front the Iraqi troops soon occupied large areas of foothills, and moved along the roads to Zakho, Dohuk and Akra. A brigade was assigned to each, and with the aid of aircraft and armour they forced their way through the road blocks, building stone sangars as they advanced. Kurdish tactics were not to allow themselves to be trapped or surrounded, and they readily abandoned their villages to avoid this, living in caves or camping in the valleys, which as it was summer was no hardship for the Kurds. As Iraq troops reached Akra and then approached Zibar and Barzan, the Kurdish rebels simply withdrew farther into the mountains where the almost total lack of roads and motorable tracks made it extremely difficult for the Iraqi soldiers to follow—but follow they did on this occasion. Zibar was occupied without opposition on the 1st August, and Barzan on the 4th, while away to the west Zakho was entered on the 10th. By this time the forces of Mullah Mustafa had been severely compressed into the northern mountains, but they mostly remained intact in their groups. By September the Government impetus had run down. The Jash, the Government Auxiliaries, reduced to a hard core of about 3,000, were mainly employed on this front to support the regular forces, but in this second offensive their value proved to be far more limited and sterile than on previous occasions.

On the central front brigade-sized columns marched in the directions of Ruwandiz and Raniya, but they ran into trouble almost immediately, as one was trapped by a force of some 400 Pesh Merga, led by Omar Mustafa, in the Ruwandiz Gorge. This action also severed Iraqi military contact between the northern and southern parts of this front, and so the other three brigades were ordered to move there to rescue the column. Fighting for the Ruwandiz Gorge lasted for eight weeks, the Pesh Merga holding out despite shelling and aerial bombardment, and it was not until the 12th August that the Gorge was once again completely in Government hands and the Kurdish rebels had been driven away. The Government drive had bogged down almost before it began.

The eastern front, that facing Suleimaniya, also had four brigades allocated to it, and the first priority was to open and clear the road from Kirkuk to that town. One brigade commenced this task, but moved so slowly that it had to be reinforced by another. The Pesh Merga held on to their positions and had to be driven from each one by shells and bombs. Again it took an eight-week fight to clear the road, after which the impetus ran down. Several acts of sabotage occurred near, and even inside, the town of Suleimaniya. During this period the Army suffered casualties.

At the same time as the second offensive was under way, a group of Merga commandos, estimated to number fewer than 200, embarked in small groups upon a campaign of sabotage and terrorism. On the 17th June two oil wells at Jambur, some 20 miles south of Kirkuk, were blown up. On the 22nd Pesh Merga commandos raided military installations at Kirkuk, and in the fighting that followed the Baghdad–Kirkuk railway was blocked for 48 hours, as were some roads. Government counter-action was savage, and the inhabitants of many of the Kurdish villages within a 25-mile radius of Kirkuk were driven out, their houses destroyed, their livestock killed and their crops burnt; in many instances the Baathist National Guard was employed to hunt down Pesh Merga commandos and harass displaced Kurdish families. On the 30th June Mullah Mustafa announced that already 167 villages had been wiped out and some 1,943 civilian inhabitants killed or wounded, including '137 children under three years of age'. Figures were always suspect, but clearly the second offensive initiated by President Aref was far more ruthless and deadly than the first offensive that had been launched by Kassem, and as throughout Iraqi aircraft had liberally strafed, bombed, fired rockets and dropped napalm, the casualties could hardly fail to be high.

In an effort to combat the sabotage and terrorist tactics of the Pesh Merga directed by the DPK, the Iraqi Government raised a small body of irregular troops known as the 'Salah ed-Din Ayyubi' Force, or the Saladin Force. It was intended that it should be composed of detribalized Kurds and local Arabs from the Mosul and Kirkuk provinces, and was trained and equipped on anti-guerrilla lines, but very few Kurds could be persuaded to join it. Being primarily designed to demonstrate the solidarity of the Kurds and Arabs within the Iraqi nation against the mountain rebels, it failed in this respect, but it became effective to a degree in the anti-sabotage field and, once it began operating, the DPK Pesh Merga subversive operations tended to subside.

There was also sabotage activity in and around Baghdad itself, where a few Kurdish commando groups began to operate during the second offensive. For example, on the 22nd June there were explosions at the Rashid Camp, which housed a number of prisoners and internees. On the 3rd July the Government announced that early that morning another attack had been made on that camp with the intention of overthrowing the régime, which had failed; Kurds, Communists and the usual whipping boy, imperialists, were officially blamed. Kurdish sabotage and terrorist tactics were smothered as the Baathist National Guard took to the streets of the capital to search out the Pesh Merga commandos. There was little deliberate sabotage in the Barzani sector. The huge Dukan Dam, across the Greater Zab, was protected by a strong detachment of soldiers and was floodlit at night to discourage Kurdish rebel attention, but Mullah Mustafa disparagingly said that his men would not attempt to disrupt the source of potential wealth he hoped to share.

Although in the opening weeks of the second offensive the Kurds almost everywhere withdrew before Government advances, they nevertheless continued to announce victory after victory, claiming to have killed or wounded hundreds of Government soldiers and auxiliaries. In one announcement the Kurdish rebels claimed to have wounded[1] 340 Iraqis, taken 720 prisoner, and captured 20 tanks, 164 machine-guns, 9 mortars, 1,000 rifles and 80 sten guns. All this was for the admitted loss by Iraqi Air Force action of 167 razed villages, 634 civilians killed and 1,309 wounded, who included women and children. While there was substance in these claims, they were considered to be greatly exaggerated. It was also probable that the Kurds, who now possessed machine-guns (a few mounted in an anti-aircraft role), brought down three or four Iraqi aircraft, but there was a stony silence on this aspect on the part of the Government, which issued no figures at all on casualties or losses at this stage.

There was no doubt that support and practical help were given to the Iraqi Government, which was predominantly Baathist in composition, by the Baathist Syrian Government, and the Syrian brigade, about 5,000 strong, which entered Iraq and took part in the second offensive on the northern front as part of the force that pushed for-

---

[1] *The Kurds* by Hassan Arfa.

ward into Zakho. On the 30th June it was widely reported that Syrian aircraft were flying with the Iraqi Air Force against the Kurds, and that one plane had been brought down, but both Governments firmly (and falsely) denied this. On the 9th July the Soviet Union expressed concern that Syrian troops were in Iraq fighting the Kurds, but two days later the Iraqi Government (again falsely) denied this. It was not until October that both the Syrian and Iraqi Governments admitted that a Syrian brigade was in Iraq serving against the Kurds. Much later, on the 21st November, the Syrian Government announced that it was prepared to send more troops to Iraq under a military agreement, but the (then) Iraqi Government, from which hardline Baathists had been purged, declined, and on the 27th it was announced that the Syrian brigade was in the process of leaving Iraq.

During the summer of 1963 Sheikh Ahmed, who still travelled between Bazan and Baghdad, despite the weight of the second offensive, became briefly disillusioned over his pro-Government stand, so he said he would take the field on the side of the Kurdish rebels against President Aref. However, this never came to anything, mainly because he could not persuade the Politburo to hand over some rifles from the DPK sector for his followers. His brother, Mullah Mustafa, would not co-operate either, so Sheikh Ahmed then relapsed into confused neutrality. Vaguely respected by the mountain Kurds, he remained the unofficial contact between Mullah Mustafa, the DPK and the Baghdad Government, all of whom regarded him as a useful tool.

Because of the unexpected heavy resistance and lack of progress of the second offensive, the Government tried to reopen negotiations with the Kurds. Contact was made, and on the 30th July 1963 a delegation led by Saleh Mahdi Ammash met Kurdish leaders, demanding first that the Kurds lay down their arms and accept the Government 'decentralization' plan. The talks dragged on until the 11th August, after which there was a pause until the 30th, when the Government demands were firmly rejected. By way of explanation, on the 18th September Jalal Talabani, who had returned by way of Persia and was with the Politburo in the DPK sector, said that it was the Government which had made the cease-fire approaches and not the Kurds, but that the Kurds were refusing to take part in time-wasting discussions.

During September the Government forces renewed pressure on all three fronts in an effort to crush Kurdish resistance before the winter.

Generally they did not make much progress, except on the eastern front, where a well-co-ordinated attack forced the DPK Pesh Merga to evacuate their Chami-Razan headquarters, which were in caves in a valley. But this was the only positive success, after which the Government military situation regressed. In October, owing to dissensions in Baghdad and a power struggle within the Baathist Party, a number of units were hastily withdrawn to the capital, weakening and even denuding fronts. The Kurds were thus enabled to advance in November and to reoccupy, often with no opposition at all, large tracts of territory from which they had been ejected earlier in the year. By the end of November, just before the winter snows blocked the mountain passes, the Kurds had occupied an area larger than they had held at the commencement of the second offensive, which included a few large villages never previously under Kurdish rebel domination. Chami-Razan was reoccupied without opposition by the DPK Pesh Merga.

In early December Army units were redeployed and the fronts again strengthened just in time to block further Kurdish rebel erosion, by which time, in the DPK sector, Suleimaniya had become completely invested by Pesh Merga positioned in the surrounding hills, while other Pesh Merga units were surging southwards towards Khanakin on the road from Suleimaniya to Baghdad. Government forces still held the main towns, but in some—such as Arbil and Kirkuk—the garrisons were largely confined to their camps and barracks, as the Kurdish rebels not only dominated such large sections of the countryside but were seeping into the suburbs. Armoured convoys, which were sometimes ambushed, were used to supply a number of beleaguered units, and as the winter snow set in and roads became impassable, urgent rations and ammunition had to be dropped by parachute, some of which drifted into rebel hands. Although a few fierce communiqués were issued by both the Government and the Kurdish rebels during January and February 1964, there was in fact no fighting of note, although a few skirmishes and ambushes did occur and Iraqi aircraft continued to attack Kurdish territory whenever weather permitted.

By this time a degree of organization, both military and civil, was becoming apparent in Kurdish territory. The influx of what amounted to over seventy Kurdish regular officers, including a brigadier,[1] who

[1] The Kurdish rebels claimed about this time that they had with them between 8,000 and 9,000 Kurds who had deserted from the Iraqi Army. There were also

had deserted to join the Kurdish National Movement, together with many long-service Kurdish non-commissioned officers, enabled the Pesh Merga to become a more efficient body with a better military command structure to control the many small and scattered units; this development proceeded faster in the DPK sector than in the Barzani sector, being forged by the more shrewd and politically motivated Politburo. It was decided to introduce formal ranks in the Pesh Merga instead of just 'responsibilities', and Mullah Mustafa grandly reassumed the rank of general, which had been bestowed on him by the Mahabad Republic in 1946. Smaller units were developed into larger and more practical ones, and already seven of battalion-size had been formed. A training school for junior leaders was established at Mahvout, 20 miles north of Chwarta, to teach partisan and ambush tactics. No new strategy or tactical doctrine was evolved, and the Kurdish military concepts remained those of a defensive war fought on the edge of the mountains against a conventional army from the plains—in other words, mountaineers pitched against plainsmen. Learning by experience, as Government troops ran into head-on fire or were ambushed, the soldiers retreated rapidly to nearby stone sangars, until aircraft or armour drove the Kurds back again. Troops secured their advance by quickly erecting these sangars as they moved forward, and as the Kurds had still not found a way to take advantage of this, they had continually to retreat farther into the mountains. T–34 tanks rumbled forward without pause to smash through roadblocks, against which the Kurds could do little. Although they had obtained a few bazookas for this purpose, they do not seem to have used them very effectively during the second offensive. The Kurdish rebels still had no artillery, and Mullah Mustafa repeatedly complained that because of this deficiency he could not mount operations against Government forces, or defend camps or localities, but this was only part of the reason. His Pesh Merga were not sufficiently trained or disciplined to attempt anything so ambitious as a deliberate attack against strongly held positions, and in particular, as time meant so little to a Kurd, there were considerable disadvantages in organizing and co-ordinating anything but the smallest raid or ambush.

A few arms were obtained, but not all that many, although the appearance of Soviet machine-guns and small arms caused specula-

---

a few Arab officers who had deserted, but usually for personal pressing reasons, such as to escape military or political justice.

tion. Shortage of ammunition remained an acute problem, and extra rounds of ammunition were awarded for acts of bravery. Other equipment was still sparse and various, the most popular items being army groundsheets and raincoats. More field radio sets were acquired, but the Kurds continued to rely mainly upon the courier relay system they had set up, runners taking messages written in Arabic. A number of radio operators were among the deserters who had joined the Kurdish rebel movement, and as the Iraqi Army still relied almost exclusively on field radio intercommunication, they were able to listen to transmissions and so were kept informed of Government military intentions and moves. In this way the Kurds were able to avoid encirclement in the first fortnight of the second offensive when the pressure was heavy.

Among the increasing number of recruits attracted to the Kurdish nationalist banner were Government officials, lawyers and doctors. Before the death of Kassem doctors had been reluctant to go into the mountains, but under the Aref régime some had been persecuted for their political views and so had taken the plunge. They were able to organize rudimentary hospitals and even an elementary health service (the main hazard was typhoid), while village and district councils brought some degree of law and order into what had deteriorated into a chaotic situation in Kurdish territory. Courts to administer justice were established, especially in the DPK sector, which increased the DPK hold on the people. In the Barzani sector less progress was made in these matters, especially as the tribesmen were unused to any other than a tribal form of control. The mountain villagers became restless and discontented as they had to give 10 per cent of their produce to help maintain the mobilized Pesh Merga and partisans. They lived meagrely by any standards, and usually only ate meat, invariably chicken or goat, once a week, while they noticed that the pampered Pesh Merga had meat three times a week and generally fared far better than they did.

In a world of turmoil, of desperate causes being lost or won on the public opinion platform, the Kurdish case was largely unheard, unnoticed and unknown; they had no effective organization or means to publicize their aims and deeds, and what exile bodies there were, such as the Committee for the Defence of the Kurdish People's Rights, at Lausanne, were almost as divorced from and out of touch with the actual revolt as were the uninformed. The DPK in particular came to realize this, and disliked the publicity flair possessed by

Mullah Mustafa. The Politburo was impressed by the way the Algerian rebellion had been conducted by the National Liberation Front, which operated from the safety of European cities, from where it could both direct the guerrilla fighters in Algeria, and also marshal world opinion against French policy. As a first step it was decided that the DPK should operate its own radio station from 'Kurdistan'. A broadcasting transmitter was purchased but it did not reach Kurdistan until after the end of 1963, so the Kurdish voice remained a low whisper on the world stage.

On the 4th October 1963 Iraq's formal announcement that it recognized the independence of Kuwait relaxed hostile pressure from the Arab League countries. In theory this meant that more troops could be moved from the south to the north to operate against the Kurdish rebels, but instead they were moved towards Baghdad, to take part in a projected plot.

The Turkish Government, on the 10th August, denied that it had interfered in Iraqi affairs in any way. This denial had been prompted, or even forced, by the Soviet Union, which had got wind of a project worked out with the Government of Iraq and Persia in secret[1] to intervene in Iraq to crush the Kurdish Revolt. Turkish troops were, with Iraqi connivance, to advance against the Kurdish rebels and to contain and crush them in the sector that reached to Mosul, while from the east the Persians were to take similar action and march on to Suleimaniya. Iraqi troops were to act in conjunction with them, the overall aim being to make a massive effort to crush the Kurdish Revolt once and for all. It is believed that DPK agents got wind of this project, and passed the information on to the Soviet Union. Mullah Mastafa's second offensive had sparked off a small Kurdish insurrection to the south of Lake Van, which was quickly smothered, after which the Turks tightened up their measures to prevent illicit cross-frontier traffic with Iraq. They were not completely successful in this and arms in small quantities continued to reach the Kurdish tribes from Iraq until well on into 1966. To the east the frontier of Iraq with Persia became easier for the smugglers and by 1966 had developed into the main transit route for arms for the Kurdish rebels. Commencing in July, the Turkish Government began to take repressive measures against the restless 'mountain Turks', which culminated in August in some twenty-five of them being sentenced to death for 'attempting to form an independent Kurdish state'.

[1] Known as 'Operation Tiger', according to Ghassemlou.

On the 28th September the Syrian Baathist Party announced its intention to work to form Syria and Iraq into a single state, a project that caused a power struggle within the Iraq Baathist Party: it also prompted the Free Officers to take action themselves. Discontent amongst military officers had been building up for some time, as in the preceding months those with Kurdish, Communist, pro-Nasser or pro-Kassem views were removed, and pro-Baathist ones, frequently far too junior or incompetent, were appointed in their places. The Army as a whole disliked the arrogance and power of the Baathist National Guard, of which some 5,000 members were active on the streets of Baghdad, and they knew that any union with Syria would have meant further purges.

During the second week of November in-fighting broke out within the Central Committee of the Baathist Party, and the Free Officers, led by General Taher Yahya and Brigadier Abdul Rahmen Aref (brother of President Aref), who commanded the 5th Infantry Division based on Baghdad, took advantage of the situation. While knowing and possibly approving of the projected plot, President Aref played a passive part. Scenting trouble, the National Guard had taken to the streets in numbers, and General Yahya ordered them to hand over their arms, which they refused to do. Arrests of National Guard leaders and prominent Baathists began on the 15th and continued on the 16th. Meanwhile, military preparations had been completed. Army and Air Force units had been brought back from the forward zones, and also from other major towns, such as Mosul and Kirkuk, into the capital. At dawn, on the 18th November, soldiers in Baghdad, led by Brigadier Aref, effected a coup, occupying all the strategic points and the radio station. President Aref announced that the Baathist-dominated Government was dissolved and that he had taken full powers for a year. Street fighting broke out in the capital as the Army turned on the National Guard, which had been roundly defeated by the time a dusk curfew was imposed, although some elements held out longer, and it was not until the 20th that the Army was in full control in Mosul and Basra. No official figures were issued for the casualties of this coup, the best estimates being between 300 and 500 killed. Hundreds were arrested, and many fled the country. As the Army assumed control, Baathist officials were ousted, and there was a purge of Baathist officers from the forces, which further weakened them, leaving them in no fit state to continue fighting the Kurdish rebels, let alone mount a winter campaign

H   113

against them. This coup had been primarily Army-instigated, as opposed to the February one, which had been mainly Air Force-instigated. The only prominent Air Force officer who took an active part was Brigadier Hardan al-Takriti, who had been promoted commander of the Air Force for his part in bringing President Aref to power.

A new Cabinet was formed on the 20th November, with General Taher Yahya as Premier, and Hardan Takriti as Defence Minister; it still contained a few moderate Baathists and one Kurd, Mosleh Nakshabandi. A fresh National Council of the Revolutionary Command was formed, consisting of President Aref, Taher Yahya (who was appointed Chief of Staff), Hardan Takriti (who became Deputy Commander-in-Chief) and the commanders of the five divisions. On the 21st November, at a press conference, President Aref stated that it was the wish of the new Government to re-establish peace with the Kurds. Although contacts had been renewed on the 18th, cease-fire negotiations did not commence at Suleimaniya until the last day of January 1964. Meanwhile, the Army, in its weakened condition, held on to its garrisons. Despite heavy snow the Pesh Merga attempted to seep forward as far as they could but generally the situation remained a heavy stalemate. Mullah Mustafa was in favour of a cease-fire, but the Politburo of the DPK, realizing how weak the Army was, wanted to fight on. Mullah Mustafa's views prevailed, and on the 10th February 1964 President Aref was able to announce that a cease-fire had been concluded and that 'Kurdish national rights would be recognized in a provisional constitution'. The national rights for Kurds were to be based on 'decentralization', and the word 'autonomy' was not mentioned. An amnesty was granted to those who had fought against the Government, and it was announced that the Government Auxiliaries, the Jash, would be disbanded. Further discussions were to be held regarding the political status of the Kurds. Mullah Mustafa ordered his followers to return to their homes—most were already there anyway—and in his Barzani sector the majority of the tribes, the Pesh Merga and partisans were in favour of the cease-fire. It was only in the DPK sector that there were opposition, suspicion and a sense of an opportunity being lost.

The second offensive, which began in June 1963, when President Aref lost patience with the ever-increasing demands of the Kurds, resulted in initial Government gains and a sizeable compression of Kurdish rebel territory, but there was a limit to how far the Army could penetrate into the maw of the mountains; as it outran its strength, a stalemate was setting in when units were withdrawn to support the October coup. The Kurds again surged forward to re-occupy the areas left empty, the removal of the Syrian brigade being to their distinct advantage too. Even after the coup, when Army units were again deployed against the rebels, they were barely able to hold on to their positions, while the Kurds continued to seep into the countryside around them until, by the time of the cease-fire in February 1964, they occupied a greater expanse of territory than they had when the second offensive began.

THE THIRD OFFENSIVE

'The Kurds, who are excellent mountain fighters, lose their
fighting qualities when fighting in the plains outside their
own tribal areas.'

Hassan Arfa, *The Kurds*

There was an uneasy and sterile period of fourteen months after the
February 1964 cease-fire; Mullah Mustafa broke with and fought the
DPK Politburo, and President Aref—his patience again exhausted—
launched the third offensive against the Kurdish rebels in April 1965.
This operation dragged on until September, when a civilian, Abdul
Rahman al-Bazzaz, became the Premier.

On the 12th February Abdul Karim Farham (a Kurd), who was
the Minister for National Guidance, stated that the cease-fire with the
Kurds had become effective in all areas, that Army units were return-
ing to their camps and that both sides were releasing their prisoners.
He also added that the Government had approved plans for repairing
damaged houses and buildings and for erecting new hospitals, schools
and police posts. In Paris, on the 14th, the Iraqi Ambassador announced that the economic blockade against the Kurds had been
lifted, and that all Kurdish Government officials and employees,
who had been suspended during the Revolt, had been reinstated. On
the 18th Radio Baghdad broadcast that Brigadier Fathi Sakalli, the
Military Governor of the city, had ordered the release of 450 Kurdish
detainees. On the 1st March the announcement was made that already over 1,200 Kurds had been freed from detention. On the 16th
the Government formally granted an amnesty to all who had supported the Kurdish Revolt since 1961. These very soothing and
heartening statements were hardly true, but were perhaps issued in
the hope that Mullah Mustafa would believe them and reciprocate.
He, however, showed no signs of being drawn.

Mullah Mustafa had accepted the cease-fire on behalf of the
Kurdish rebels on condition that the Government recognized Kurdish national rights under a new constitution and, of course, granted
a full amnesty to all who had been involved. He acted much against

the wishes of the DPK Politburo. He knew he lacked its support and, indeed, he feared that the DPK would not stop hostilities in the DPK sector. After waiting a few days he held a press conference to explain his point of view. Speaking as much as anything to mollify the Politburo, he affirmed that it was merely a cease-fire and that the Kurds would not lay down their arms and return home until all their political demands had been met. He added that besides the bare cease-fire agreement there had been another written one, which embodied in secret clauses the precise conditions that were to be settled in later talks. In this connexion he said that he had been invited to go to Baghdad but he declined, suggesting instead that the Premier, Taher Yahya, came to meet him on his home ground at Raniya. The Kurds were continually trying to bring President Nasser into their negotiations. Although it seems certain that Nasser had played no part at all in bringing about this cease-fire, Mullah Mustafa insisted that Nasser had offered to act as mediator, but that there had been no need for his assistance—a statement that was not confirmed by the Egyptians or any other source.

So far, despite the basic disagreements between Mullah Mustafa and the DPK, relations had been smooth enough to prevent an open rupture, and so both were able to present a united façade to the world. This had been largely due to the fact that both were busily and quietly consolidating their own power bases, and each side thought it could use the other; which to a large degree was correct. During the previous months Mullah Mustafa had striven to gain control of all the units of Pesh Mergas in the field, while the DPK had concentrated upon gaining political influence and building an infrastructure it could use to impose itself on the people. The DPK was using typical and proved Communist techniques. While a cease-fire was of undoubted benefit to the DPK, the Politburo was by no means happy about it; it had to acknowledge Mullah Mustafa as the national Kurdish leader and accept his decision in this matter, simply because the DPK still had hardly any grass roots support while Mullah Mustafa had plenty, but it intrigued against him behind his back. In March Jalal Talabani and some members of the DPK went to Cairo to try to enlist President Nasser's support on their behalf against Mullah Mustafa, but they got only vague promises. This move naturally became known to President Aref who, of course, strongly suspected what the true position was. He gave an empty promise to implement some of the Kurdish demands almost immediately, but loudly said that if the DPK acted contrary to Mullah Mustafa's orders he would send the Iraqi Army against it.

Basking in this oblique support from the Iraqi Government, Mullah Mustafa flexed his muscles. When, instead of quietening down in the DPK sector, the Pesh Merga there began to move aggressively northwards, he hastily came to terms with certain tribes (including elements of the Zibari, Baradosti and Herki tribes), which he had coldly ignored so far, or which had been friendly with the Government. These tribal elements occupied a sort of 'no-man's-land' between the DPK sector and the Barzani sector. By separating the two they had made contact between them difficult and prevented open friction. These new alliances, brought about because of Mullah Mustafa's now generally accepted role as the only Kurdish national leader of any stature, curbed the DPK for the time being. From a prestige point of view it became unpopular for any Kurd with a sense of nationalism to fight against him. As the DPK Pesh Merga were suspect and disliked, tribes involved with them were only too pleased to help Mullah Mustafa bring them to heel. Back-stage intrigue continued; when Jalal Talabani went to Teheran, without Mullah Mustafa's knowledge, during the visit of President de Gaulle to Persia, Mullah Mustafa quickly got on the bandwagon and claimed that the Kurdish Revolt had full CENTO backing—another statement completely without foundation.

On the 3rd May a new provisional constitution for Iraq was promulgated, which guaranteed the Kurdish 'nation rights within the Iraq national unity', a vague statement that immediately displeased the DPK Politburo, which now demanded autonomy as the absolute minimum it would accept. A few days later Mullah Mustafa submitted a memorandum to the Government asserting that the new constitution neither recognized the Kurdish right to autonomy nor established a democratic régime. He added that thousands of Kurds were still imprisoned by the state, that no Army units had been withdrawn from the forward areas, that the Jash (the Government Auxiliaries) had not been disbanded, and that Kurdish officials and those with Kurdish sympathies had not been reinstated.

In an interview[1] on the 12th June, President Aref said that he no longer advocated union with Egypt (as he had in 1958), and that the Tripartite Agreement of April 1963 between Egypt, Syria and Iraq was a failure. Talking on the Kurdish problem, he said that Mullah

[1] With *Le Monde*.

Mustafa constantly assured him of his loyalty, but that members of the DPK, who surrounded Mullah Mustafa, were 'warmongers, spies and agents', whom he thought Mullah Mustafa would have liked to suppress if he could. On the 18th a new Government, composed mainly of Baathists and Nationalists, was formed by Taher Yahya.

On the 5th June talks commenced at Raniya between a delegation led by Taher Yahya, the Premier, and another led by Mullah Mustafa, at which Mullah Mustafa demanded a democratically elected legislature and a separate executive for Kurdish territory. Yahya proposed that this should be postponed until 1967, when the next general election was due. At this conference Mullah Mustafa refused the Government demand for the dissolution of the DPK and the surrender of Communists who had taken refuge in Kurdish territory. However, it was agreed that the new provisional constitution should be amended to recognize the existence of the 'Kurdish people whose development would be parallel with that of the Arabs in Iraq'. It was also agreed that the disbandment of the Jash should be accelerated (it had not even started), that Army units should be withdrawn from certain areas, and that the use of the Kurdish language in schools in Kurdish territory should be developed. Taher Yahya and Mullah Mustafa parted, but the Government took none of its promised steps—it just sat back and watched smugly as fighting broke out amongst the Kurds themselves. Meanwhile, on the 14th July, President Aref announced the formation of the Arab Socialist Union of Iraq, into which all legal and approved existing political parties and organizations were to be merged: the DPK and the ICP were excluded. President Aref at the same time nationalized all the banks in Iraq and many of the large commercial concerns.

The February cease-fire caused the breach between Mullah Mustafa and the DPK to widen as their divergent views clashed. Mullah Mustafa was content with the cease-fire, hoping he would be able to secure most of his demands by negotiation in due course, but the DPK was of the firm opinion that to continue the fighting would have specially benefited the Kurds as the Army was weak and the Government unsteady and, indeed, unsure of precisely how much support it commanded within Iraq. Although Jalal Talabani had no success on his mission to President Nasser, he seems to have achieved more from his visits in the spring (of 1964) to Teheran. The Persian Government did not want to see a strong, united Iraq, which might rival or outshine Persia in Middle East affairs, and so was happy to poke a sly finger into the Kurdish pie. As the Persian Government had large numbers of Kurds to administer it did not want them bitten by the same bug of nationalism that was infecting the Iraqi Kurds, so it was also content to see the Iraqi Kurds at one another's throats. Whatever promises of support Talabani had obtained from Teheran, they must have been sufficient to encourage the DPK Politburo to ignore Mullah Mustafa's instructions and to state that it was determined to fight on.

Mullah Mustafa relied almost exclusively for his power on the conservative tribal sheikhs and elders. On the other hand, the DPK Politburo, like the Central Committee, consisted almost entirely of urban intellectuals who were not only far removed from the tribes in thought, sympathy and contact but who, as openly as they dared, advocated social reforms that cut straight across normal tribal authority. In parts of the DPK sector they had made a start by putting some of their ideals into practice in an attempt to socialize the people. In May the Pesh Merga, with its new-found allies, began to push southwards into the DPK sector. As they advanced they dissolved the 'elected peasant councils' that had been established by the DPK, which brought Mullah Mustafa more support from the sheikhs. He also abolished certain 'agrarian reform measures' which the DPK had introduced into their 'liberated areas'. In June Ibrahim Ahmed organized a DPK Congress, which condemned Mullah Mustafa's attitude to the Government, the continuing cease-fire, and Mullah Mustafa's defence of feudal and tribal order in Kurdish territory. This prompted Mullah Mustafa to more active measures. During the first week in July a force estimated to amount to some 2,000 Pesh Merga, mostly Barzanis, and some 500 partisans, under the command of Lokman Barzani (Mullah Mustafa's son), advanced towards Mahvout where the DPK had its headquarters near the Persian border on the road towards the Persian town of Baneh. Mullah Mustafa acted from a position of strength, mainly because the Iraqi Government, anxious for peace, had agreed to deal only with him in negotiating with the Kurds, and partly because of the actions of his Pesh Merga in restoring authority to the sheikhs in the DPK sector, many of whom had been neutral so far. Now, as they were interested in being on the winning side, they openly backed Mullah Mustafa. First of all Mullah Mustafa called upon the DPK to hand over its arms to him, but the Politburo refused flatly. Although the DPK sector was run on typical Communist 'committee lines', that is, by the Politburo acting together, Ibrahim Ahmed tended to take the lead in political matters, while Jalal Talabani tended to emerge as the field commander. The DPK still had about 650 Pesh Merga.[1]

As Lokman and his force advanced, the DPK evacuated Mahvout and, crossing the Lesser Zab River, moved over the Persian border towards Sardasht, to settle down near Dulekan, about 12 miles over the frontier. There the Pesh Merga remained under Talabani, while Ibrahim Ahmed went off to Teheran to negotiate with the Persian Government. The Persian authorities unsuccessfully attempted to disarm the DPK, but Talabani resisted, saying they were about to recross into Iraq. Sheikh Ahmed of Barzan now came ineffectually into the picture again, as he attempted to mediate between Mullah Mustafa and the DPK.

While in Persia, Jalal Talabani managed to recruit another 100 Pesh Merga from the southern part of the Persian Kurdistan province. When Ibrahim Ahmed returned from his fruitless journey to Teheran, the reinforced DPK force attempted to go back to Chwarta, in Iraq, by way of the main road to Suleimaniya, but on crossing the frontier it was ambushed by Lokman's Pesh Merga with disastrous results. In the fighting some 200 Pesh Merga deserted the DPK and went over to Lokman, while the remnants fled back into Persia. After a few days they concentrated near Baneh, where they were disarmed and placed under surveillance. The Iraqi Government protested against such a subversive and potentially dangerous body being so near the border, so the Persian Government moved it first to Saqqiz and then to Hamadan. This internecine victory won, in the last days of July Mullah Mustafa convened a DPK Congress—he was still nominally the Chairman—at Raniya, which pledged him full support and expelled the Politburo and eleven other members from the DPK Central Committee. July 1964 had been a bad month for the DPK but, despite its failure to take over the leadership of the Kurdish Revolt by force, it remained active. Its sympathizers overseas, especially in Syria, Lebanon and Lausanne, continued to support its cause rather than that of Mullah Mustafa. With most of the virile members of the DPK Central Committee in exile, Mullah Mustafa was able to strengthen his grass roots support and his hold on the Kurdish political machine which was fast developing in Kurdish territory.

[1] Some reports mention 630 Pesh Merga, some of whom had been forcibly conscripted.

Striking while the iron was hot, Mullah Mustafa organized another, larger and more comprehensive Kurdish Congress at Raniya
in mid-September, which voted him full powers to lead the Kurdish
Revolt. Mullah Mustafa had undoubtedly emerged triumphant from
the attempt to usurp him. However, at this Congress he was invited
to recall the DPK dissidents from Persia and to reabsorb their energy
and talents in the Revolt. Sheikh Hama Rashid, of the Baneh (Persian) tribe, became the mediator. He brought Omar Mustafa, of the
Politburo, to Iraq for talks with Salem Abdullah Yousefi, who then
went back to Persia to fetch Jalal Talabani for talks with Mullah
Mustafa himself. Again, old Sheikh Ahmed came into the picture.
Eventually Mullah Mustafa agreed that most members of the DPK
could return to Iraq, provided they came under his orders and
ceased all political activity. He stated that he was assuming both the
political and military leadership of the Kurds, and he promised to
resume hostilities against the Government if autonomy was not
granted in a reasonable time. Ibrahim Ahmed, the Secretary, and
Said Aziz, a member of the Politburo, were among those excluded
from this offer, which in principle was accepted by Talabani on behalf of the DPK. There were many DPK reservations and only a
trickle slowly returned from Persia to join Mullah Mustafa and work
under him. The main group hesitated and remained where it was.

As usual, the Government of Iraq was having an uneasy and unsettling time, and in September 1964 it had to cope with an attempted
coup by the exiled Baathist leader, Ali Saleh Sadi, who had returned
secretly to Baghdad. On the 5th aircraft were to have attacked Baghdad airport as President Aref was leaving to attend an Arab summit
meeting at Alexandria, and also to have beaten back any armour or
ground troops that moved in to support Army elements loyal to the
Government. This plot was discovered in time and suppressed, and
over 3,000 Baathists were arrested. Major-General Ahmed Hassan
Bakr, Major-General Hardan Takriti, and Colonel Latif were
alleged to have been the military ringleaders, and were either retired
from the Army or removed from their posts.

The Government's persistent refusal to grant any concessions, or
to implement any of its promises to the Kurds, forced Mullah
Mustafa to adopt a more radical line of action in his negotiations.
On the 11th October 1964 he openly accused the Iraqi Government
of failing to begin the projected economic, rehabilitation and building programme in Kurdish territory, and of systematically 'Arabiz-

ing' the oil-producing regions of Arbil and Kirkuk. He alleged that Government expenditure in the north had been restricted to projects calculated to strengthen the Army's positions and that of the Jash, that 'thousands of Kurdish families' had been expelled from Kirkuk, and that '37 villages in the Arbil region' had been forcibly evacuated and taken over by Arabs. Mullah Mustafa also criticized the Government for forming the ASU, the single legal political party, which Kurds were not permitted to join. He also renewed demands, which he had put forward in 1963, for a regional Kurdish executive and legislature, a virtually autonomous Kurdish militia, proportional division of oil royalties, the appointment of a Kurdish Vice-President and the inclusion of Kurdish representation in the Government. He also proposed that if any federal union was established between Iraq and any other country, as had been mooted from time to time, Kurdish territory should enter on equal terms with the other countries concerned. Lengthy talks on these demands brought no response from the Government.

Mullah Mustafa had hoped that President Nasser would persuade President Aref to come to an agreement with the Kurds, but he had been particularly uninterested. The Kurds therefore made contacts with political parties not officially recognized by Aref and thus barred from the ASU—such as the Communists and the Baathists—in the hope of obtaining their support, but again they had little success. On the contrary, contact with the out-of-favour Baathists tended to have an adverse effect, making the Government even more intractable and suspicious. On the 4th October Mullah Mustafa held another large Kurdish Congress at Raniga, which decided that, as the Government had done nothing whatever to fulfil its promises to the Kurds made seven months previously, they should take practical action to form themselves into an autonomous territory with an autonomous administration. By the end of the month the Kurds had set up a Kurdish Legislature of some 43 members, a Council of the Revolutionary Command to direct the war, and an Executive Committee of 11 members. Mullah Mustafa emerged as the dominant personality, placing his own nominees where he wanted them. Within a few weeks virtual autonomy was established in about three-quarters of Kurdish territory, which was divided into five administrative districts, each with its own military governor and financial and judicial administration.

The Kurds were clearly getting restless at the delaying tactics of the

Government, and from mid-October onwards there were several minor clashes between the partisans and Government troops, which were mainly indecisive. These continued spasmodically into November, when they subsided, being dampened down by the onset of the winter snows. Mullah Mustafa was still reluctant to reopen hostilities, and he kept his impatient Kurds on as tight a rein as he could. The skirmishes had mainly involved partisans over which he had only minimal influence.

On the 14th November 1964 a new Government was formed by Taher Yahya, the object being to implement the proposed union of Iraq with Egypt, and personalities were shuffled accordingly. This proposed union upset the Kurds, who felt that if it materialized their national aspirations would be completely obliterated, and they increased their political agitation for speedy autonomy. Mullah Mustafa had difficulty in restraining Kurds with more extreme views, who were fast losing patience.

After the unsuccessful coup of Ali Saleh Sadi in September 1964, the Baathist Party, weakened as so many of its members had been arrested, was driven underground. Such as remained at large were dissatisfied with the Party leadership and at a secret congress in December they expelled it and elected a fresh Central Committee, which adopted a new programme. Calling for a democratic régime to replace that of Aref, the congress condemned the war against the Kurds, supported a large measure of autonomy for them, and demanded an alliance of 'Nasserite' forces, by which it meant the Baathist Party, the ICP, the DPK and other 'progressive' elements. But Mullah Mustafa and the Kurds were suspicious of this hand held out to them, and continued to ignore and distrust the Baathist Party.

The repeated calls for a return to democracy touched President Aref on the raw, causing him to make empty placatory gestures. On the 6th January 1965 he formally abrogated martial law, which had been in force since the 1958 revolution, and on the 26th he relinquished the special powers given to him in May 1964 when he had been authorized to exercise all the powers of the NCRC. But this meant little or nothing, as censorship remained and the country continued to be held down by a military dictatorship. As there was still no sign of the Government making any attempt to implement its promises, Mullah Mustafa, in a last effort to avert further hostilities, submitted new and much more moderate proposals to President Aref. They included the use of the Kurdish language in Kurdish

124

territory, the appointment of Kurdish officials to posts in Kurdish territory 'where possible', and the maintenance by the Kurds of an armed force of between 2,000 and 3,000 men as a guarantee of good will. No mention was made of any division of oil revenues. The Government abruptly rejected these moderate demands without discussion, and then began a press campaign against Mullah Mustafa personally to discredit him. President Nasser wanted the Kurdish problem over and done with, and on the 22nd February sent a message to Mullah Mustafa urging him to surrender. During March the Government attitude hardened, and it decided to launch a spring offensive designed to crush the Kurdish rebels completely. On the 3rd April Taher Yahya, the Premier, visited President Nasser to inform him beforehand of the projected third offensive. Nasser expressed stern disapproval, as he regarded a reopening of the Kurdish war as weakening the Arab front he was trying to build against Israel, especially at a time when he had large forces tied up in the Yemen.

On the 3rd April armoured vehicles entered Suleimaniya to deal with disturbances caused by the Kurds, and in the fighting that developed the Kurds claimed that sixty people were killed and several hundred wounded. This was only a preliminary. The Government had made up its mind, and on the 5th the third offensive was launched all along the 250-mile arc of the Kurdish front, from Zakho to Khanakin, with some nine brigades, amounting to over 40,000 troops. The now familiar pattern was again repeated, with the Iraqi Army, with air cover, initially advancing without much difficulty to occupy a number of towns and large villages, which included Raniya (where Mullah Mustafa had his headquarters) and Barzan. Under pressure the Kurds withdrew farther into the mountains, and retaliated by night raids, ambushes and attacks on communications, while in riposte Government forces bombed villages and burnt crops with napalm.

In the former DPK sector Government troops ran into hard opposition, and there was fighting for such centres as Panjwin, Chwarta and Mahvout, which was generally indecisive; but there were reports of Government casualties and reverses. The Iraqi Army was unable to penetrate deeply into these mountains. On the 7th July it was reported that the Kurdish rebels were using field artillery and bazookas for the first time, which made the Army more reluctant to attempt further advances. Following these failures, Iraqi security forces took harsh measures against sections of the Kurdish civilian population in Suleimaniya, Kirkuk and Arbil, in which some Kurds were killed, many were wounded, hundreds were arrested, and houses were destroyed.

In the Barzani sector, cautiously poking their way northwards, Army units reopened the main roads and reoccupied most of the places they had taken in the first and second offensives, and which they subsequently had to evacuate. After being driven from Raniya, near Galala, Mullah Mustafa established his headquarters in the mountains on the road running westwards from Ruwandiz to the Persian border, which he managed to maintain throughout the third offensive. He saw the value and necessity of a formal headquarters.

This time there was some measure of co-operation between the Governments of Iraq and Persia. Combined military operations took place against the Kurds in the areas of the common frontier, but they failed to seal the border. Although Persian troops generally contained the Kurdish rebels, in at least one instance, in July, they suffered a reverse with casualties near Kala Diza, which was just on the Iraqi side, a few miles north of Chwarta. On the other main frontier the Turks did their best to maintain a strict blockade against the Kurds, thickening the minefields and increasing the number of border posts and patrols, but relations between the two Governments were extremely cold and were not improved when, on the 28th July, an Iraqi aircraft bombed and machine-gunned a Turkish border village, killing one person and wounding eight.

The Iraqi Army was incapable of maintaining the momentum against the Kurds for long, and it soon slackened off. The Kurds were thus enabled at least to remain where they were, and in some cases even to advance and force the Government troops back a little way. Generally, August was a month of military stalemate, and by September all the energy of the third offensive had drained away. Plagued with many political intrigues, the Government was too preoccupied to concentrate solely on the war against the Kurds which, incidentally, coincided with a revolt by the Yazidis—the 50,000-strong sect of 'Devil Worshippers' who lived in a region some 50 miles to the west of Mosul—which caused several Army brigades to be diverted from the Kurdish front.

The third offensive had begun quietly, almost secretly, and the first public admission that a campaign was under way was made in a speech by President Aref on the 14th June. Thereafter bombastic communiqés were issued by both sides. The Kurdish rebels claimed that during the first month of the fighting large numbers of Kurdish regular officers and soldiers deserted from the Iraqi Army,[1] and this was to some extent confirmed on the 5th May, and again on the 24th, when the Government promised that deserters who returned to their units would be pardoned. During this offensive the Government lost one of its most valuable allies, Sheikh Mohammed Lowlani, leader of the 30,000-strong Lowlan tribe, who declared his allegiance to the Kurdish nationalist cause. A few tribes, or parts of tribes, were still fighting against Mullah Mustafa, and a few more still stood aloof and were not yet allied with him, although most of the Zibaris and Bara-dostis, his traditional enemies, had come out on his side against the Aref Government. A hard core of some 3,000 Jash remained, con-sisting of a mixture of mercenary detribalized and urban Kurds and those from sections of tribes which for a variety of reasons were fighting for the Government—a situation indicating that the Kurds were not yet nationally united, although they were very much more so than they had ever been before.

A sense of isolation, increased by the resumption of hostilities against the Kurds, hastened reconciliation between the remainder of the DPK personnel exiled in Persia and Mulla Mustafa. During the summer practically all returned to Iraq and were either given back their former posts or were assimilated into the new Kurdish ad-ministration that had been set up. The DPK sector sprang into life again as the Pesh Merga loyal to the DPK took up its former posi-tions. Jalal Talabani had already returned and had early made his peace with Mullah Mustafa. In May 1965, when visiting London as Mullah Mustafa's representative, Talabani gave a press conference at which he alleged that the Iraqi Army had used poison gas against the Kurds[2] on at least two occasions, and also that both America and the Soviet Union had refused to supply arms to the Iraqi Govern-ment while the fighting continued. The allegations of the use of poison gas were quickly refuted by Abdul Rahman al-Bazzaz, the Iraqi Ambassador in London.

In April a DPK spokesman said that it would support the Baathist Party's call for a coalition government. Since the nationalization measures of July 1964 the ICP had adopted a more conciliatory

[1] Reports said 'including 75 officers'.

[2] Allegations that the Egyptians were using poison gas against the Royalists in the Yemen were rife at about this time, and probably Talabani thought it might make a good propaganda point. No evidence was produced to substantiate these allegations.

attitude towards President Aref, and in April 1965 changed its policy after a majority decision of its Central Committee to collaborate with all political groups opposed to President Aref and to give complete support to the DPK. In May 1965 the UAR-Iraqi Unified Political Command met in Cairo for the first time under the joint chairmanship of Presidents Nasser and Aref, but in their final communiqué no mention was made at all of the Kurdish problem.

The policy of crushing the Kurdish Revolt with a heavy hand, formulated by President Aref and Premier Taher Yahya, was generally supported in the Cabinet, although there was a strong minority dissenting group of 'Nasserite ministers', led by Fuad Rikabi, which was firmly opposed to this war. Rikabi, who also opposed any settlement with the ICP, criticized the lukewarm application of the 1964 nationalization laws and wanted to accelerate the union of Iraq with Egypt. He also hoped to use the Arab Socialist Union, the only permitted political party, as the instrument to achieve this purpose, while President Aref saw, and wanted to use, the ASU as the basis of his power and support. Aref favoured a more conciliatory policy towards the large (about 55 per cent of the 8·25 million people in Iraq) and very conservative Shia Moslem community, which looked towards Persia for spiritual guidance and denounced union with Egypt. The Shias were also against the war with the Kurds and the nationalization measures.

At the beginning of the third offensive there had been differences in the Cabinet between the Nasserite ministers and those who favoured prosecuting the war against the Kurds. In May Rikabi was placed under surveillance, but all this was kept quiet and did not come to light until the 1st July, when Abdul Karim Farham, Minister of National Guidance and Secretary of the ASU, was, while on a visit to Cairo, suddenly dismissed from the Government.[1] In protest Fuad Rikabi and five other Nasserite ministers resigned, which simply meant that this small hard core of resistance to the Kurdish war was removed. Although he wished to remain independent of Egypt, President Aref intended to stay in the forefront of the Arab movement against the Israelis. On the 9th June he announced that Iraq had placed a certain number of military units at the disposal of the Arab Unified High Command, and that he would send others to Egypt to accentuate co-operation between the armed forces of the

---

[1] The reported reason for Farham's dismissal was his criticism of the Shia institution of temporary marriage.

signed, but it took some months of negotiations before the French Government announced (in December) that it was prepared to supply arms and aircraft to Iraq. An Iraqi military mission visited France.

In the Kurdish rebel camp during the second half of the year there was rising discontent with the Government for not implementing the Twelve Point Programme. Friction was caused between Mullah Mustafa, who counselled patience, and the dissident DPK element which, growing in strength and voice, demanded stronger action. During the summer and autumn Jalal Talabani and many of his followers had quietly infiltrated back, with or without Mullah Mustafa's blessing and pardon, into the southern part of the former DPK sector, managing to establish themselves fairly firmly in the vicinity of Suleimaniya, at Chami-Razan, Dukan, Chwarta and Mahvout, and in the course of doing so clashing on several occasions with the Pesh Merga and partisans loyal to Mullah Mustafa. Despite these activities, Talabani continued to maintain contact and communications with both Mullah Mustafa and the Iraqi Government. He was working hard to establish himself and his faction firmly as an independent Kurdish political force, with the ultimate aim of eclipsing Mullah Mustafa.

In December an unsuccessful attempt to assassinate Talabani was reported. Elements in the Government, not interested in placating the Kurds, saw the value of encouraging Talabani in his ambition, hoping he might both cause internal dissension and, conceivably, oust Mullah Mustafa and become a Government puppet.

The other body active during this period was the Saladin Force, still mainly composed of Arabs but with a slowly increasing proportion of Kurds. It was suspected that even at this stage Talabani was in touch with this Government-sponsored body, and that he had infiltrated a number of his dissident DPK followers into it. Such Kurds as served in the Saladin Force were either strongly politically motivated urbanized ones, or those from tribes still not reconciled to the leadership of Mullah Mustafa. During December the Saladin Force, which was trained in anti-sabotage and guerrilla tactics, was employed in the region of Kirkuk where several instances of sabotage occurred.

FINAL UNSUCCESSFUL OFFENSIVES

'The Kurds have no friends.'

Kurdish proverb

The Iraqi Government's efforts to obtain arms from France were seemingly about to be successful when the Kurds put a damper on the negotiations. A French military mission had visited Iraq in January 1968, and on the 7th February President Aref paid an official visit to France, when he obviously hoped to be able to conclude a satisfactory arms agreement. Apprehensive in case any modern French weapons might be turned against the Kurds as well as the Israelis, on that date Mullah Mustafa sent a letter to President de Gaulle, asking him not to supply military material to the Iraqis until the Kurdish problem had been solved, and expressing his fears as to potential misuse. At this moment there was a wave of sympathy sweeping across France for the Kurdish cause and a statement, signed by a number of prominent Frenchmen, appeared urging that French arms should be supplied to the Iraqi Government only on the condition they would not be used against the Kurds. On the 9th[1] President Aref denied that any French arms given to Iraq would be used against the Kurds, and put down any such suggestion to Zionist propaganda. This suggested reservation on the French side had some effect and when President Aref ended his visit on the 10th the official communiqué made no mention of the possible supply of arms. On the 14th it was stated in the French National Assembly that the question of arms for Iraq did not arise at the moment, although the following day it was reported that the French Government had agreed to supply that country with seventy armoured cars. This was one of the few occasions when Kurdish propaganda and overseas agitation proved effective, but the Kurds had left it far too late to develop this technique; they should have commenced such activities

[1] On the 8th President Aref made some unfortunate anti-Zionist remarks, which gave him adverse publicity, there being a strong pro-Israeli sentiment in France at the time despite official French policy.

146

in 1961 when, had they done so, the course of the revolt and the outcome might have been more beneficial to them. Even at this late stage they did not seem to appreciate fully the value of sympathetic world opinion, or have much idea how to cultivate and develop it.

Eventually, on the 6th April, it was reported that a contract had been signed in Baghdad for the supply of fifty-four Mirage aircraft to the Iraqi Government. However, this was cancelled shortly afterwards, partly because the Iraqi Air Force objected to the protracted training required by Mirage pilots, and partly on the grounds of excessive cost, it being estimated that a Mirage cost about three times as much as a MiG–21. Provoked by the French attempt to supply arms to Iraq, the Soviet Union had come into the picture again, doing its best to dissuade the Iraqi Government from buying French aircraft. Indeed, the Soviet Defence Minister visited Baghdad in March 1968 to call for more co-operation between the armed forces of Iraq, Syria and the UAR.

The non-implementation of the Twelve Point Programme continued to cause unrest amongst the Kurds, which gave the Government some anxiety. Special precautions, including the use of the Saladin Force, were taken in the Kirkuk area after the December 1967 incidents of sabotage. There was a spasm of Kurdish dissidence in the Arbil sector in April, when on the 12th and 13th 'outlaw elements' were officially stated to have attacked a military patrol, killing four soldiers and six civilians. Dissident DPK members were suspected, although this was never formally substantiated, Talabani hoping that Mullah Mustafa would be blamed and accused of being incapable of controlling his men. This and other incidents were engineered deliberately to embarrass Mullah Mustafa. Angry at the re-emergence and growing strength of Talabani as a political and military force, Mullah Mustafa had already taken some steps to assert his authority. His Pesh Merga clashed with Talabani's followers on several occasions, and on the 5th March it was reported that nineteen people had been killed in 'interfactional fighting' in an area just to the south of Raniya. On the 25th June two Kurdish ministers, Abdul Fattah al-Shali (Development of Northern Iraq) and Ihsan Shirzada (Housing), resigned, followed on the 6th July by the resignation of Abdul Karim Fuad (Agriculture), the last Kurd in the Government—all because they could not agree with Premier Yahya's policy towards the Kurds.

During the latter part of 1967 discontent with the Yahya Government had risen steadily, and in January 1968 six of his ministers resigned and had to be replaced. President Aref admitted a general anti-Government trend. On the 16th April a petition asking for the removal of Premier Yahya and for a stronger government was submitted to President Aref by a group of retired officers of various political persuasions, including Baathists, Nasserites and Nationalists, and which included General Ahmed Hassan Bakr, a previous Baathist Premier, and Major-General Abdul Aziz Okeili, a former Defence Minister. On the 6th May it was announced that elections, fixed at three-yearly intervals in 1964 (but put back one year in 1967), would be further postponed until 1970. Political frustration continued to mount. On the 12th July Premier Yahya resigned, but President Aref rejected demands from senior officers, serving and retired, that Yahya should leave the Government, and instead asked him to form another, which he did on the 16th.

On the 17th the President Aref régime was overthrown by a bloodless Baathist coup, led by General Bakr. At dawn armour and infantry surrounded the Presidential Palace, meeting no resistance as the Presidential Guard was in the plot. General Bakr telephoned President Aref, calling on him to resign and surrender, and when no answer was received warning shots were fired at the Palace. In a further telephone conversation, after being guaranteed a safe-conduct, Aref surrendered. He was put on an aircraft to London. Premier Yahya and others were arrested, and Bakr became President of Iraq. It was confirmed that the coup was the result of a conspiracy of right-wing Baathists and younger military officers who, disconcerted and disappointed by the part played by the Iraqi armed forces in the Third Arab–Israeli War, had come together to form a secret organization called the Arab Revolutionary Movement. President Aref and his Government had not been able to win and hold sufficient popular support, owing to unrest following defeat by the Israelis, dislike of too much Egyptian influence, alleged widespread corruption, and to some degree—although this should not be over-emphasized—failure to settle the Kurdish problem.

On the 19th July Colonel Abdul Razzak al-Nayef, a former Director of Intelligence and one of the prominent leaders of the coup, formed a Government composed mainly of right-wing Baathists and Nationalists, which contained three Kurdish ministers, but the Kurds did not take up their appointments. Two of the three, Ihsan Shirzada and Mohsen Dizayi (the latter was allocated the Portfolio of Development of Northern Iraq), were supporters of Mullah Mustafa. The third was Mosleh Nakshabandi, a supporter of Jalal Talabani. At a press conference on the 24th July Premier Nayef said that his Government was preparing a plan for the Kurdish problem and that Mullah Mustafa had been informed of his Government's views. The Twelve Point Programme was not mentioned. On the following day Premier Nayef rescinded the press censorship law of December 1967, thus allowing newspapers to appear again. Mullah Mustafa adopted a reserved attitude towards the Nayef Government, and in an interview[1] said that 'as long as military dictatorships succeed one another in Baghdad, no solution to our problem will be possible. The national rights of the Kurds and the integrity of the Iraqi state will be assured only when a genuine democracy is established'.

Differences between the Baathists and the Nationalists led to the sudden eruption of disputes within the Government, and after a Cabinet meeting on the morning of the 30th July, at which there had been violent disagreement, an armoured force took up position around the Presidential Palace and members of the Baathist National Guard militia reappeared on the streets in large numbers to occupy key positions in the city. In the afternoon Premier Nayef was arrested and put on a plane for Morocco. Ibrahim Abdul Rahman al-Daoud, the Defence Minister, who would have supported Nayef and probably been able to muster enough force to prevent such a coup from becoming successful, had left the previous day to inspect Iraqi units in Jordan; he too was arrested and flown to Rome.

On the 31st President Ahmed Hassan Bakr formed a Government predominantly Baathist in character, which retained portfolios for the two pro-Mullah Mustafa Kurds, Ihsan Shirzada and Mohsen Dizayi, who had still not taken their seats, but dropped Mosleh Nakshabandi, who supported Talabani. Power was now concentrated mainly in the hands of President Bakr, Hardan Takriti, the Defence Minister and a Deputy Premier, and Saleh Mahdi Ammash, also a Deputy Premier. The reappearance of the Baathist National Guard militia, which had conducted such a reign of terror in the capital in 1963, caused alarm, and a number of prominent political personalities went underground. As the political chaos subsided, the militia was withdrawn from the streets and Baghdad settled down again. During August the Government released many Communists

[1] *Le Monde* of 29th July 1968.

in the hope that they would strengthen the moderates in the ICP, which was becoming extremely militant, but the principal Communist leaders were still kept in detention. President Bakr hoped eventually to bring the Communists into a National Front, so that he would then be able to exercise a measure of control over them, but he was unsuccessful as the Communists refused to accept any of his political conditions.

On the 3rd August the new Revolutionary Command Council announced that it was ready to settle the Kurdish problem on the basis of the Twelve Point Programme, and that a Government delegation would soon leave Baghdad to make contact with the Kurdish leaders. On the following day the Government said that it would implement the language and cultural points, and the day after (5th) that it would grant an amnesty for all Kurdish soldiers and civilians, this amnesty to include a provision that those who had deserted from the Army or the police would not be required to surrender any arms or ammunition taken at the time. The Government also stated that 300 political prisoners detained by the previous Yahya Government would be released but it did not say how many Kurds. All this meant little in practice and was largely designed to keep the Kurds quiet for a while, as the main priority and preoccupation in Iraq was the Palestine problem, coupled with the anxiety that Iraq should play a full part in all Arab councils in the struggle against Israel.

The agile Jalal Talabani made and developed a good liaison with the Bakr Government, so successfully that it insisted that Talabani be included in all talks on Kurdish matters, which did not amuse Mullah Mustafa at all. Although both Mullah Mustafa and Talabani continued to communicate with each other, neither had any illusions about the other's intentions and ambitions; each watched for an opportunity to use or outwit the other. During September Talabani and his followers strengthened their hold on parts of the former DPK sector. Realizing what was happening, Mullah Mustafa sent units of his Pesh Merga south to prevent this area being taken from him. By this time Mullah Mustafa had managed to bring practically all the Pesh Merga and partisans firmly under his control, but he was less certain of the loyalty of the Kurdish political and administrative superstructure, which contained many younger urbanized Kurds, out of sympathy with old tribal traditions, and so he had to tread carefully in certain aspects. Although Talabani did not accept the expulsion of himself and many of his followers from the Politburo, Central

Committee and the DPK, the cold fact was they had been roughly bundled out, and the DPK, with an entirely reconstructed Central Committee, was controlled by Mullah Mustafa. It is no longer accurate to describe Talabani and his followers as being part of, or in, the DPK, albeit they could be described as a dissident splinter group of that organization.

Talabani's followers decidedly got the worst of the several encounters they had during October with the Pesh Merga of Mullah Mustafa; they were being rapidly squeezed out when, at Talabani's request, the Government stepped in and sent troops to his aid. President Bakr saw that Talabani might have his uses, and would be of even more potential value to him if he were able not only to maintain his positions in the field but improve them and spread out into other parts of the former DPK sector, adjacent to the Persian frontier. Talabani was now virtually fighting on the Government side against Mullah Mustafa. In support of Talabani, aircraft of the Iraqi Air Force bombed Kurdish villages, causing Mullah Mustafa, on the 18th November, to present another memorandum to the UN alleging that the Iraqi Government was attempting genocide of the Kurds, and asking for a UN mediator to be appointed.

On the 3rd January 1969 the Government launched an offensive against the Kurds, using about 60,000 troops (some twelve brigades), the object being to break through to and remain in occupation of the stretch of territory from Ruwandiz in the north to the Suleimaniya area in the south. The military planners remembered that two years previously their sudden winter offensive had all but achieved a breakthrough in the Panjwin area, so it was decided to try a similar tactic on a much broader front. Once again the Government troops gained surprise, and although the offensive lasted only three weeks until the severe winter conditions halted the momentum, the shaken Pesh Merga were tumbled back in several places and made to abandon others, but they put up enough resistance to prevent the Government troops from achieving their objective. However, a few places of tactical importance, including Panjwin and Kala-Diza, quite close to the Persian frontier, were taken and held. During this offensive the followers of Talabani were helped and encouraged to reoccupy some of their former positions, including Chwarta and Mahvout. On the 4th February President Bakr announced that the Government had put into effect most of the provisions of the Twelve Point Programme; while by no means true, the statement was meant to calm the situation. Pompously, Bakr said: 'We are looking forward to seeing an increasing number of our Kurdish brothers believe in a peaceful settlement as a result of the course the progressive Government is taking.'

Extremely bad weather precluded operations during February, but Mullah Mustafa was quick off the mark on the 1st March, opening an offensive mainly aimed at driving Government troops out from the positions they had just occupied. Confused fighting followed, lasting for several weeks, in which the Iraqi Army slowly gave ground and withdrew from the mountains, leaving the Kurdish rebels once again in possession. Mullah Mustafa had marked the opening of his offensive with a flourish by shelling some Iraq Petroleum Company installations near Kirkuk, but this had been a diversion, the main weight of his attacks being to the east into territory adjacent to the Persian frontier. The Government replied by intensive use of aircraft to bomb Kurdish villages, and of the Saladin Force.

Sheer exhaustion on both sides mainly caused the fighting to die down in June. At the end of that month a communiqué was issued by Mullah Mustafa claiming that the Kurds had reoccupied Kala-Diza and Panjwin, and that all the Iraqi Army's assaults to recapture them had been repulsed with the loss of about 1,000 killed and wounded—all for fewer than 150 Kurdish casualties. He alleged that Iraqi aircraft had dropped napalm and nitric-acid bombs on thirty-seven Kurdish villages, killing 730 civilians. This fighting had forced Talabani out into the open on the side of the Bakr Government. So, giving up all pretence of loyalty to Mullah Mustafa as the leader of the Revolt, he turned his coat and began recruiting Kurds to fight against the Pesh Merga. In this project he had some success. Although figures are suspect and unconfirmed, it was generally estimated that he raised a mercenary force of 1,000 to fight under his command for the Government, although some put its strength at fewer than 500, this not including those Kurds he had integrated into the Saladin Force. On the 9th April an unsuccessful attempt—attributed to Talabani's followers—was made to assassinate Mullah Mustafa, when his vehicle was ambushed and fired upon.

The tailing off of the Government campaign against the Kurds in June, although largely necessitated by exhaustion and Pesh Merga resistance, was also partly attributable to an external and an internal factor. The external factor was the sudden renewed eruption of bad relations with neighbouring Persia, this time over conflicting claims to the Shatt-al-Arab that separated the two countries in the extreme south, the Persian Government having abrogated the 1937 Treaty dealing with the administration of that waterway. On the 20th April there had been reliable reports of Persian troops massing near the southern end of their joint frontier. Alarmed, Iraq had to make counter military moves, which meant withdrawing forces from Kurdish territory. It also brought the dispute before the UN (on the 30th). At the same time the Bakr Government began forcibly repatriating Persian subjects resident in Iraq, which in turn caused Persia to complain to the UN. As so much tacit assistance had been given to these Kurdish rebels by Persia, together with a large measure of obstruction and non-co-operation, the Iraqi Government now undoubtedly felt a degree of smug satisfaction at being able to hit back, even in this small way. Previously (14th January 1969) the Shah, wanting to gain paramount influence over the Persian Gulf states, had officially reiterated his claim to Bahrein. The internal factor was one that plagued several Arab countries after the Israeli victory, that of independent Arab guerrilla organizations springing up over which governments had extremely limited, or no, control at all. Iraq was no exception; on the 17th April a left-wing newspaper, *Al Nida*, gave some details of guerrillas in Iraq and stated that the people objected to their presence. To neutralize this problem before it got out of hand the Baathist Party, which had held a comprehensive ten-day conference in February that had discussed such items as Israel, defence and Arab guerrillas, formed its own guerrilla organization, known as the Arab Liberation Front, and kept it under the firm control of the Party. The ALF provided the necessary emotional safety valve for the passions of the moment and helped to squeeze out other rival bodies that would not accept Government instructions—a process that took several months and diverted attention and energy from the Kurdish problem.

Initially the Syrians had carried out a propaganda hate campaign against the Bakr régime in Iraq, but a change of Government had meant a change of policy that brought the two countries closer together, and on the 15th March 1969 an Iraqi brigade entered Syria ostensibly to strengthen that country against possible attack from Israel. On the 26th March Hafez Assad, the Syrian Defence Minister, called for union between Egypt, Syria and Iraq, and also for the reunification of the Syrian and Iraqi Baathist Parties. Later, on the 2nd June, President Bakr, in a more modest voice, called for the political and military union with Syria, that should be expanded to include all Arab countries bordering Israel. Meanwhile wholesale arrests of political opponents and a series of dramatic 'spy trials', followed by public executions, began in late 1968. On the 12th December President Bakr said that 'not a single agent or saboteur will remain on Iraqi soil'. The trials continued throughout 1969, which made for unease, fear and mistrust in Iraq.

Most of 1968 had been spent in reorganizing the shaken Iraqi armed forces and in trying to restore their morale and confidence in themselves, which was achieved to a sufficient degree to launch the brief winter offensive in January 1969. As negotiations for French aircraft and arms had not been successful, Iraqi eyes again turned to Moscow. An Iraqi military delegation visited the Soviet Union in September 1968 to ask for aircraft, artillery and armour, and another visited Moscow in May 1969, but Soviet material arrived slowly. By June the Army strength was still in the region of 70,000, the new conscription law of the previous month (decreeing that all males over nineteen years of age serve in the armed forces for twenty-three months—a considerable tightening up of the existing lax rules) had not yet taken effect, and the Air Force still had about 10,000 men. It was estimated that the Army now had some 575 tanks, including many T-55s and T-54s, and that the Air Force possessed some 18 bombers, 215 fighters (mainly MiGs), 40 transport aircraft and 40 helicopters. In both numbers and material the picture seemed to be quite good, but there remained the basic weakness of the Iraqi armed forces caused by the drastic officer purges which had not been stayed during the Bakr régime, and which left them weak, inert and lacking in purpose and energy. Although nominally still retained in divisional formations, Iraqi's brigades were operating more loosely and independently in a far more flexible and practicable manner. The Iraqi Army was composed of some sixteen brigades, of which three were armoured; of these, three were stationed in Jordan, one in Syria, and another four had been moved towards the southern part of Iraq opposite the Persian frontier. Allowing for at least three brigades to garrison the capital to protect the ruling régime, this would seem to leave only five to operate against the Kurds, so it is quite understandable that President Bakr, whose twelve-brigade winter offensive had made little indentation on the Kurdish military position, began to negotiate secretly with the Kurds in June. He also had to reckon with the probable demands of the Palestine problem, and the fact that the total Persian armed forces numbered over 180,000 and had over 250 aircraft in support, including modern US types.

The Bakr Government began talks with Kurdish representatives in June 1969 which were held at Beirut, in the Lebanon, with Michael Aflak, Secretary of the Baathist Party, as the unofficial mediator. These negotiations were in secret, but gradually information about them leaked out, or was deliberately fed to the press, causing speculation. Stalemate was early reached as the Kurds would not discuss anything less than the Twelve Point Programme, so while still keeping the talks going the Government decided to take military action again.

By denuding the Persian southern front of troops, the Government was able to muster some ten brigades, which it used to launch an August offensive on a wide front, the main objectives being Zakho (which had been held by the Kurds for many months), Ruwandiz, Raniya, Kala-Diza, Mahvout and the Panjwin areas. During the last week of August and the first two weeks in September, under cover of artillery fire and supported by aircraft, five columns pushed slowly into the mountains, being opposed by some 15,000 Pesh Merga and partisans, to whom were later added other tribal warriors as Mullah Mustafa sent out the rallying call. It was reported that the Government forces were supported by 30,000 irregulars, but this is considered to be a false estimate, as apart from about 2,000 Jash and the 1,000-strong Talabani unit, it is doubtful whether even the uncommitted tribes would be keen on fighting against Mullah Mustafa.

In the north the Iraqi Army column completely failed to reach Zakho and had to fall back again. Another column suffered harsh setbacks near Arbil, and another near Dukan, while the fighting around Ruwandiz, Kala-Diza and Panjwin soon bogged down inconclusively. After a final fortnight's flash-in-the-pan, when fresh efforts were made to assault Kurdish positions, the offensive died down in October, having accomplished none of its original objectives. The Kurds claimed that on the night of 20th–21st September, for example, units of their Pesh Merga made a successful night attack on an Army camp near Dukan, in which they destroyed thirty tanks and three days later (24th) they also claimed to have beaten back an attack in the Panjwin region led against them by Talabani and his mercenaries. Talabani was by this time absolutely committed to the Government side. The Kurds allege that during September the Iraqi

Air Force made 120 attacks on Kurdish villages, forcing some 200,000 villagers to take refuge in the mountains.

Belatedly the Kurds were beginning to appreciate the value of atrocity stories for consumption by world opinion. Reports reaching the West on 3rd October alleged that Government troops had massacred the entire population of two villages, killing ninety-nine old men, women and children in one, and sixty-seven in the other. Another Kurdish allegation was that on the 16th August near the village of Dakan[1] to the north-east of Mosul, Government troops, finding some Kurds hiding in a cave, started a fire at the entrance and that only three of seventy persons escaped. The Iraqis quickly denied these allegations, but the smear had been made.

The other aspect that was accentuated during this unsuccessful offensive was the rather ham-handed Iraqi attempt to prove Persian involvement when, on the 18th September, it was announced over Baghdad Radio that thirty Persian soldiers had been killed and fourteen others captured by the Iraqi Army while trying to recross the frontier back to their own country, in an area where the border was controlled by Kurdish rebels. The report alleged that those captured had confessed that they were regular soldiers sent to infiltrate into Iraq. On the following day the Persian Foreign Minister flatly denied any Persian intervention, adding that 'certain elements of the population in the frontier regions, whose families are the object of almost daily bombing and napalm attacks by Iraqi forces engaged against Mullah Mustafa's troops, may have been driven to participate in the fight without the Persian Government's knowledge'. This tended to confirm that, while the Persian Government turned a blind eye to Kurdish tribesmen crossing from Persia into Iraq, there was no official involvement, Persian troops correctly keeping to their own side of the frontier. The Iraqi Government seemed unable to obtain evidence to the contrary, and no captured Persian soldiers were ever exhibited to the foreign press. On many occasions Iraqi shells had fallen on Persian soil and Iraqi aircraft had attacked villages on the edge of the Persian border, but if the Persian Government retaliated it did so by proxy—through its own Kurdish tribesmen.

Realizing that the armed forces were making little impression on the Kurdish rebels, but were simply exhausting themselves for no territorial gain, the Bakr Government representatives, still secretly meeting those of Mullah Mustafa in Beirut, stated that certain con-

[1] Near the Dakan Dam: not to be confused with Dukan.

cessions would be made to the Kurds. These mainly concerned the reorganization of the Kurdish administrative departments at Suleimaniya, Arbil and Dohok, and the mixed Arab–Kurdish administrative department of Kirkuk, which were given a small measure of autonomy. A little later other concessions, chiefly in the educational and publishing spheres were made, but in practice they did not amount to much, and failed to draw Mullah Mustafa, who on the 21st December stated that not only was he dissatisfied with these gestures but he would not negotiate with the Bakr Government any more. His boast that he was in control of half the Kurdish territory of Iraq, with a population of 1·2 million, brought a sharp retort from the Iraqi Ambassador in Paris (on the 28th) to the effect that the total population of the Northern Province was only 1·5 million, of whom 500,000 were non-Kurds. He claimed that Mullah Mustafa had only 'succeeded in disturbing a narrow strip of frontier, thanks to Teheran's complicity'.

This was yet another attempt to implicate Persia openly. Iraqi chagrin at Persia's attitude was understandable and there was little doubt that a large combined Persian–Iraqi military operation could have solved Iraq's Kurdish problem, as also might permission to use tracts of Persian frontier territory to enable Iraqi forces to strike at the rebels from the rear and to encircle them. The year 1969 ended on the now familiar note of Government failure to come to terms with the Kurds and of military stalemate, the Government later estimating that during the year the Kurdish fighting had absorbed nearly 30 per cent of the total budget. It was admitted that the autumn fighting had been at the cost of over 1,000 Government casualties, which were alleged to have been mainly incurred by the Jash and Talabani's mercenaries.

President Bakr, still holding office as Premier, realized the strength of Mullah Mustafa's forces. At last he was convinced that the Kurdish problem could not be solved by military means alone, and that a peace settlement by negotiation was the best answer. This decision was additionally prompted by the open antagonism of Persia and by Iraq's involvement in the Palestine problem, aggravated as that had become by the rash actions of some of the independent Arab guerrilla organizations. In December President Bakr sent Fuad Aref, a Kurd and former minister, to contact Mullah Mustafa, who insisted that any agreement reached with the Government must be registered with the UN to ensure implementation. Ignoring this condition, Bakr

157

detailed Saddam Hussein Takriti,[1] a Vice-President and prominent Baathist leader, to head a Government delegation. On the Kurdish side the chief negotiator was to be Mahmoud Osman, who had risen to become second only in importance to Mullah Mustafa himself, his official position being Secretary-General of the Executive Bureau of Kurdistan.

During 1968 and 1969 there had been a complete reorganization of the political and administrative structure in Kurdish territory, and the nomenclature and jargon had been up-dated. The Executive Bureau of Kurdistan had evolved from the old Politburo of the DPK, from which all the traces of the Talabani influence had been eliminated, and the old DPK Central Committee had evolved into the Revolutionary Command Council of Kurdistan. The other principal Kurdish negotiator was Mohammed Mahmoud, who had been a Pesh Merga front commander in the Ruwandiz area and was now a prominent member of the Executive Bureau of Kurdistan.

On the 21st January 1970 it was announced that a plot to overthrow the Government had been detected and crushed the previous day, and that all the conspirators had been arrested. The only casualties were two Government soldiers, who were given a state funeral. This attempted coup was led by right-wing and pro-Western elements in the armed forces, which were increasingly disturbed by the Government's pro-Communist policy and its proposals for a peace settlement with the Kurds. It had been led by Major-General Abdul Ghani al-Rawi, and it was later reported that forty-four people who had been involved were executed. Apparently the Government had known of this plot for three months and so was able to feed its own agents into the conspiracy; these eventually assembled the some 300 officers who were intimately concerned, persuading them to walk unarmed into a trap. The Bakr Government blamed both the Persian Government, alleging that it had supplied machine-guns and ammunition, and the American Central Intelligence Agency. The Persian Ambassador in Baghdad was expelled from the country.

On the 24th January the Revolutionary Command Council issued a statement affirming that it supported the Twelve Point Programme of 1966 and desired to settle the Kurdish problem peacefully. To create the necessary atmosphere it granted an amnesty to all soldiers and civilians who had taken part in the Revolt and said they could

[1] Not to be confused with his cousin, Major-General Hardan Takriti, who was the Minister of Defence.

retain any arms and ammunition they had—something that had been stated on previous occasions without effect, mainly perhaps because Iraqi Governments were not trusted. The Bakr Government also called upon local authorities to reinstate all officials who had been dismissed for taking part in the Revolt, but this was another gesture that was regarded with cynicism. The attempted January coup had demonstrated just how many internal enemies the Bakr régime was faced with, and so it became all the more anxious to make a good and lasting peace with the Kurds and win their popular support. At the end of the month a Kurdish delegation was invited to Baghdad to begin talks with Saddam Hussein Takriti. It took time to dispel the air of unreality that usually descended on such negotiations. There had been so many fruitless rounds of meetings and talks in the past that each thought the other was not serious, but was merely playing for time for devious reasons. However, on this occasion the Government meant business.

For several weeks the bargaining was hard and long, but at last both sides were agreed, and on the 11th March 1970 an Armistice Agreement was signed despite opposition from Saleh Mahdi Ammash, Baathist Minister of the Interior. Signing the document for the Kurds were Idri Barzani and Masood Barzani, two of Mullah Mustafa's sons. The following day President Bakr announced that the war against the Kurds had ended, and that the Government recognized the right of the Kurds to cultural autonomy and national equality, the actual conditions being much on the same pattern as the Twelve Point Programme. The Kurds had gained a 15-point peace settlement that guaranteed almost complete autonomy. Some of the other main clauses provided that there should be a Kurdish Vice-President, that Kurdish was to be one of the two official languages, and that Kurds were to be represented in the Government, Army, police, legislatures and universities in proportion to their numbers. Precise details were not given, but were to be worked out jointly. In a broadcast Mullah Mustafa gave his acceptance and approval. He had again triumphed, as the Government negotiators had wanted to bring Jalal Talabani into the discussions, but the Kurdish delegation had objected and they had given way. The ambitious, but unfortunate, Talabani had been sacrificed to expediency. President Bakr said that, 'This solution is . . . a permanent solution that will last for ever,' while Saddam Hussein Takriti, negotiator and Deputy Chairman of the Revolutionary Command Council, stated that it was 'Not a temporary truce, but a complete, substantial, political and constitutional solution ensuring brotherhood for all time between Arabs and Kurds.'

Many of the Communists in the Mullah Mustafa camp—and there were a large number—wished to have a secure Kurdish autonomous base for their own ultimate purpose and use. They had encouraged the Kurdish negotiators to hold out for hard terms, and Mullah Mustafa had to persuade them to modify some of their extreme demands. Although pressing hard for whatever advantages they could prise from the Government, the Kurds also badly wanted peace. They were influenced by such factors as general war-weariness of the people, who had suffered economic blockade and bombing for nine years, and the morale-shaking (although unknown) number of casualties[1] that continued to be incurred even though no official military offensive was in progress for much of the time. For example, it was admitted (in February 1970) by the Kurds that they had lost over 100 Pesh Merga since October 1969. The younger element of urbanized Kurds now in key positions in the DPK and the Kurdish administration were anxious to come to terms with the Baathists. In short there was as much, if not more, satisfaction in the Kurdish camp as in Government circles. The future suddenly appeared bright and promises of economic rehabilitation and development seemed to be on the point of materializing, especially when Mohammed Mahmoud, a negotiator, was appointed Minister for the Development of Northern Iraq and given responsibility for initiating and carrying through these measures. It was planned that the Kurds would obtain their autonomous regions within four years, the boundaries to be defined by census within a year.

On the 18th March a nine-man Committee of Arabs and Kurds was formed under the Chairmanship of Murtada al-Haditha, a senior member of the Revolutionary Command Council, to supervise and work out details of the agreement. On the 29th the Baathist Government was reshuffled and five Kurds, all acceptable to Mullah Mustafa, were brought into it. On the 10th April Mullah Mustafa denied that he ever intended to establish an independent Kurdish state, and said: 'I

[1] Kurdish casualties, especially of civilians from aerial attacks, had been very heavy. As no reliable records were kept it is not possible to assess them accurately, Kurdish figures being largely inflated guesses. One set of figures that may have a greater degree of accuracy was that issued in February 1970, when Mullah Mustafa stated that about 13,000 families were receiving Kurdish assistance after losing their breadwinner since 1960.

only defend my people's rights within Iraq. From now on we, as people attached to the policy of the Iraqi Government, will do our best to improve relations established between Iraq and Turkey and other countries.' It seemed that now all was going smoothly, as indeed it was for a while.

On the 3rd July Kurds gathered at Gallala, the frontier village where Mullah Mustafa had long had his headquarters, mainly to elect a Kurdish nominee for Vice-President from the (now) seven-man Executive Committee of Kurdistan. Habib Karim was chosen. A review of progress towards implementation of the peace agreement was made; it was generally considered to be slow but satisfactory. The main lack of progress had been in respect of the promised mixed National Assembly, which was to have contained 25 per cent Kurds, but it was recognized that the Baathists were having difficulties because of their general unpopularity with other parties and factions. Some anxiety was felt because the Bakr Government had given warning that there might be more arrests and more show trials, as they might provoke and provide fuel for attempted coups. It was feared that if the Bakr Government were toppled any successor might not be as sympathetic towards Kurdish aspirations. It had been agreed that Mullah Mustafa's Pesh Merga, now officially at a strength of 21,000 (many partisans having been hastily incorporated into the ranks), would be employed on some form of frontier duties. The Talabani mercenaries who had fought against the Kurdish rebels remained a moot point, the Government wanting to employ them as a sort of provincial security force, but there were objections from Mullah Mustafa, who was not keen to have such an armed body, potentially hostile to him, in or near Kurdish territory at all. Administrative boundaries were being resolved, the Kurds were to have a weekly and a monthly language newspaper, and the Kurdish festival of Nawrouz was accepted as an official holiday.

A new provisional constitution, which took Kurdish claims into account, was promulgated on the 16th July, after which the rosy glow tended to fade as the final settlement was held up by two main issues that remained in dispute, that of the Vice-Presidency, and that of the city of Kirkuk.

The name of Habib Karim, who had been chosen at the Kurdish conference in July to be the nominee for Vice-President of Iraq, was put forward, but suddenly the Bakr Government dug its heels in and refused to accept him, or indeed to give him any other appointment, because of his previously friendly relations with the Persian Government. It was true that at this moment Iraq was on extremely bad terms with Persia, as both countries were vying hard for influence in the Persian Gulf, but this did seem an unusual step and an unnecessary stumbling-block, as the post in reality was a constitutional prestige one rather than one that carried immense political weight, or influence where Arab Iraqi interests were at stake.

The other stumbling-block was the city of Kirkuk. While the Kurds did not demand that they should administer the oil installations in the area, but merely asked for a proportionate share in the oil royalties, they did want that city to be their new Kurdish capital. The people in the countryside around were mainly Kurdish, but the city was not, having a mixed population of about 40,000 Arabs, Turkomans, Assyrians and Kurds—the exact proportion of each was in dispute. Mullah Mustafa had been granted the Kirkuk province, but not the city. The Government felt it would be inconvenient for an autonomous Kurdistan to have its capital in such a disputed city, and so it prevaricated. Initially there was to have been a plebiscite on the 26th October, but when the Government began bringing back members of the Assyrian community who had fled from Kirkuk during the Revolt to counter-balance the Kurdish families that were being quickly moved in for voting purposes, Mullah Mustafa loudly complained that Arabs were being encouraged by the Government to flock into the city. Amid these recriminations the plebiscite was postponed indefinitely on the 16th October.

Although by the end of 1970 implementation of the March Agreement was slowing down, Mullah Mustafa had achieved much, and from his position of strength, as compared with the Bakr régime, he could afford to play a waiting game. He had given nothing away, he still physically occupied Kurdish territory (the maximum he had ever held in extent), his force of Pesh Merga was armed and intact, and he had been 'allowed' to retain his heavy weapons, some 140 guns of various sorts, for the simple reason that the Government was not able to take them away from him. He still had his radio station—according to the terms of the agreement it had been silent since March 1970 —which he had exploited hardly at all, but which could be opened up again more effectively by a younger, urban generation of Kurds who appreciated the value and techniques of propaganda and public relations.

Much of Mullah Mustafa's strength lay in his political machine, the reshaped and slightly reorientated DPK, purged of Talabani influences, which was then under his control. He realized that with younger Kurds of radical and socialist views rising within it, the DPK might not always remain so docile, but he had outwitted subversive political elements before, and remained confident that he would continue to be able to do so. The DPK official programme included demands for an autonomous Kurdistan, economic growth and development, and democratic rights for all in Iraq. The DPK wanted peace as it was convinced there was mineral wealth in the mountains that could be exploited to the benefit of Kurdistan; it also wanted to develop agriculture, especially tobacco growing, and tourism. The DPK was concerning itself primarily with the future of an autonomous Kurdistan, and was not obsessed with the Palestine problem, as the Arab Iraqis were, or with confrontation with Persia over influence in the Persian Gulf or the Shatt-al-Arab. The Kurdish problem remained but in the background, as the fire had gone out of it, although the muscles and backbone remained: the Kurdish Revolt had faded out in 1970.

RETROSPECT AND PROSPECT

'Have patience and the body of your enemy will be carried past your door.'

Arab proverb

The Kurdish Revolt of 1961–1970 was confined to Iraq, and so involved only a comparatively small proportion of the Kurdish race. Thus it could perhaps more properly be known as the Iraqi Kurdish Revolt, as it was not of an international character. Although there were rumbles of sympathy and minor eruptions in both Turkey and Persia, they neither helped nor affected the Revolt at all. As soon as the scope of the Revolt became clear to Turkey it closed the mountainous section of its frontier with Iraq, and brought in strict measures to prevent cross-border traffic (such as clearing a narrow strip of territory of people so that Army patrols could shoot any unauthorized persons in the prohibited zone), although it did not actually put a stop to arms smuggling until 1966.

While relations between the Governments of Turkey and Iraq were never good, the Turks saw the danger of the spirit of the Kurdish Revolt spilling over into their country and affecting discontented elements of the over 3 million 'Mountain Turks'. They feared that a surge of aggressive nationalism could sweep quickly through the Kurdish race as a whole, and they realized the difficulties there would be in coping with such a gigantic insurrection, especially if the Kurds obtained wide international recognition, sympathy and practical support, and were able to interest the UN in their cause. Turkey was dealing with its Kurdish problem quite well, and was strong enough to smother incidents of insurrection and sweep the remains under the carpet. Turkey's excellent relations and good standing with NATO nations, for example, would have taken a hard knock had a huge Kurdish 'running sore' erupted in full view of a sanctimonious and critical world; so Turkey developed a rigid attitude of no knowledge of, no help for and no encouragement of the Iraqi Kurdish Revolt.

Persia on the other hand took a different view and in the initial stages of the Revolt could barely conceal its smug self-satisfaction at the predicament the Iraqi Government found itself in. For the first three years or so news of Kurdish rebel activities and, of course, Iraqi Government failures to quell them, was broadcast over Persian radio stations and given in some Persian newspapers. In the fifteen years that elapsed from the demise of the Kurdish Mahabad Republic Persia had harshly, but effectively, brought its over 1 million Kurds under firm Governmental control, after which large sums of money were spent on economic development schemes in Kurdish areas (unlike Iraq, which hardly spent anything on such projects in Kurdish territory) and efforts were made to soften the hard, empty life in the mountains and to integrate the Kurds into the Persian economy. In the background was an army, nearly 200,000 strong, with formations strategically placed, supported by over 200 modern aircraft, instantly ready to stamp out any Kurdish dissidence. From this position of complacent strength the Persian Government smiled pityingly down on the Iraqis with their difficult Kurdish problem, never thinking it necessary to impose such rigid frontier curbs as did Turkey.

Having originally assumed that the Kurdish Revolt would have been put down by Iraqi armed forces, or at least brought under some measure of control, by 1964, the Persian Government began to have second thoughts, especially when it was seen that Iraqi military efforts hardly made any indentation, and that Mullah Mustafa was actually uniting diverse and mutually hostile tribes under his banner, something not thought possible. Momentarily the Persians had doubts as to the wisdom of allowing arms and supplies to continue being sent to the rebels by way of Persian territory, and of allowing their border tribes to give active support. Steps were taken to close the frontier with Iraq and to reduce cross-border traffic, but they were not very effective. The Persian radio ceased to carry news about the Revolt.

The Persian Government had so far been cynically confident in the knowledge that most if its own Kurdish border tribes were bitterly antagonistic towards Mullah Mustafa and his Barzanis, particularly as he had walked over them in such a roughshod manner when escaping in early 1947. Suddenly the Persians became anxious: Mullah Mustafa had become a hero and a national Kurdish leader, and the DPK was forging a political framework and seeking to impose it upon the Kurds in conjunction with him. It seemed as though the Kurdish people were proving history wrong and uniting, and that Governments would no longer be able to play one off against the other. If this surge of nationalism seeped over into Kurdish Persian territory, the Persian Government and its armed forces would have a very different and difficult problem on their hands.

However, this mood and these fears passed when fighting between Mullah Mustafa and the dissident DPK broke out, and British announcements of pending withdrawal from the Persian Gulf were made. Persia's own prosperity depended upon the export of oil, which was carried in tankers down the Persian Gulf, and so with the prospect of a British vacuum in this region, the Shah determined to make his country the paramount one in the area. Amongst other moves he renewed his claim to Bahrein. This policy brought him in sharp opposition to Iraq, which was also flexing its puny muscles and wishing to assume a paramount role in the Persian Gulf. Relations between Persia and Iraq steadily deteriorated as the two countries immediately squabbled over administrative rights on the Shatt-al-Arab, and a military confrontation developed that lasted until after the end of the Kurdish Revolt. It was to Persia's advantage that the Kurdish Revolt in Iraq continued to divide the country and drain it of resources and strength, so the supply of arms and stores across the Persian border, which had never really ceased, was allowed to resume its former proportions. It must be emphasized that this volume was never great, as witnessed by the comparatively small number of arms in rebel hands when the Revolt ended, a factor that was dictated by the amount of money the Kurds could raise to buy them. The Kurdish rebels had no sponsor country willing to give arms or send them on credit; all transactions were in cash, and lack of money was a bigger disadvantage than has been generally appreciated. The attitude of the Persian Government remained outwardly correct, and its military forces stayed strictly on their own side of the frontier—no evidence to the contrary was ever satisfactorily produced—but the Government used obstructive and 'blind-eye' tactics in relation to the activities of its Kurdish tribes in support of the rebels. Many of the rebel wounded, for example (there being practically no medical facilities in Kurdish rebel territory in Iraq), were taken across the border into Persia where a number of field hospitals and aid centres had been established to look after them. The Persian Government partially admitted this by saying that it provided only humanitarian facilities.

To the north the Soviet Union ranged aggressively against the forward CENTO line of defence and kept its southern frontier securely shut, so its tiny number of Kurds (just over 100,000) were decisively cut off from their fellow Kurds in the south. In any case, they were separated from Iraq by some 200 miles of rugged Persian and Turkish terrain; even had they wished, and had it been politically possible, they could not have made any direct contribution to the Revolt. It was often alleged that the Soviet Union supplied arms to the Kurdish rebels and did its best to stir up dissidence, but there is little evidence to support such charges. Soviet weapons appeared in rebel hands, but they had been bought on the black markets of the Middle East and smuggled in through Persia.

The some 400,000 Kurds in Syria likewise had no influence on, or contact with, the Kurdish rebels. Since 1958 they had been a repressed and underprivileged minority which had to behave itself. As frequently the Governments of Iraq and Syria were in accord with each other, strong military action could be taken against them if they rose in revolt or actively assisted the rebels. At one stage Syrian aircraft and troops were fighting with the Iraqi forces against the rebels in Iraq, and at another there was an Iraqi brigade in Syria, so opportunity to help was not there. Additionally, there were large expanses of open country between the north-eastern corner of Syria, where the Kurds were domiciled, and Kurdish rebel territory, dominated by Iraqi armour, which made contact dangerous and difficult.

Despite the pious hopes of sympathizers that the Kurdish Revolt might take root and spread until the whole of Greater Kurdistan became alive with insurgency, the cold fact is that there was little chance of this ever materializing. Geography militated against it, as Greater Kurdistan was an inland mountainous area, a convenient international buffer, upon which had descended, since World War I, the heavy indelible mesh of international frontiers which firmly boxed the Kurdish people off into sections, forcing them to look outwards to alien Governments and cultures, rather than allowing them to congeal into a united nation. Earlier political maturity might have enabled the Kurds to form a national state after World War I, perhaps with an access to the Mediterranean, and to have gained international approbation when Turkey, Persia and Russia were weak and when the outright support of a strong, friendly (or scheming) foreign power might have been won.

The Kurdish Revolt produced no new strategy or techniques of war: it was the case of the lightly armed, mobile tribesman in his mountains being able to hold at bay conventional, road-bound military formations, which were at an increasing disadvantage the farther

167

they pushed into such terrain, where an almost complete absence of motorable roads made them vulnerable to partisan-type actions such as ambushes. As long as the tribesmen used 'hit-and-run' tactics and did not become involved in rigid defensive positions, they had the freedom of the countryside, while Government forces, locked up in isolated garrisons that often had to be supplied by air, operated from tenuous roadways. Lacking heavy weapons, military organization and discipline, the tribesmen were at a corresponding disadvantage whenever they ventured out of their mountain homeland down on to the plains, where fire-power, armoured mobility and conventional forces came into their own against what was little more than an armed mob.

Previous to the Revolt there had been no unity between the tribes, and Governments had been able not only to play one off against the other but to bribe them to fight each other, which meant that there were always tribes prepared to fight their fellow Kurds whenever they rose in insurrection or became difficult. As Mullah Mustafa acquired stature as a national leader the tendency to band together developed until it became distinctly unpopular for a Kurd to fight against Kurdish nationalism; a few continued to do so right until the end of the Revolt, but they were a decreasing number. The Jash by 1965 had been reduced to a small hard core of less than 3,000, mostly detribalized Kurds who, having committed themselves unthinkingly to the Government side in the early days, were not able to change over easily, or others who had been ejected from their tribes or for other reasons could not return home again. The Jash, who had been mainly just caught up in events and had no political motivation, sank to less than 2,000 and then dwindled rapidly in 1970 until the problem of their resettlement was almost solved by their virtual disappearance. The Kurds who fought for Jalal Talabani, estimated to be over 1,000 in 1970, were another matter as most had become politically indoctrinated or motivated. Talabani,[1] for a while under house-arrest in Baghdad, and his colleagues kept them intact and up to strength for political bargaining purposes.

Once the Pesh Merga was organized, the Iraqi Army was faced with a standing military force, which was something entirely new. Formerly, after fighting ceased, the tribesmen dispersed to their

---

[1] At the time of writing Talabani has again come to terms with Mullah Mustafa and lives in Gallala in Kurdish territory under surveillance. However, many of his supporters are allowed to hold posts in the autonomous Government.

homes, and so Government forces were able to reoccupy—usually without opposition—any territory lost, or which they wished to penetrate, as the tribesmen needed time to remuster for action, and meanwhile tribal territory was comparatively defenceless. The presence of the Pesh Merga remedied this defect, and prevented the Iraqi Army units from taking advantage of lulls in the fighting to reoccupy strategic points, towns, villages and roads.

Extensive use of aircraft against the rebels caused fear, casualties, damage to houses and an immense refugee problem but it had no decisive influence on the course of the war, even though the rebels were without anti-aircraft weapons until the last two years of the Revolt. Caves in the mountains and valleys provided ample shelter, and once the aircraft had gone the people came out again, a fact which confirms that such partisan-type wars cannot be won by aerial action alone or—if the rebel leadership is resolute—even influenced by it to any great degree. No new military lessons or techniques were learnt or evolved in the Kurdish Revolt; but a number of age-old ones were emphasized.

The Revolt itself was really a long stalemate, once the Pesh Merga was organized, punctuated by a few violent spasms. There was little prospect of the Iraqi Army being able to break it, and it lasted so long because Iraqi Governments and forces were weak. Since its birth, after World War I, Iraq as a country has been struggling desperately for unity, stability and a place in the Arab sun, and to successive Governments, each primarily concerned with its own survival, the Kurdish problem has always been seen as one of a tedious, perverse minority which would not integrate. In predominantly Arab Iraq the Kurds have always been a side-issue, a 'running sore', that governments have got used to, only occasionally losing patience to scratch at it viciously, invariably causing more pain than cure. Arab Iraqi priorities have always been elsewhere, and Arab Iraqi eyes have seldom looked northwards to the Kurdish mountains for long.

Successive Governments would have dearly liked to quash the Kurdish problem once and for all, but their armed forces were incapable of doing so. The Army, remaining at a strength of about 70,000, was small enough indeed to combat some 15,000 Pesh Merga and to put down the Revolt in such a vast mountainous region. Its morale suffered from the large number of Kurdish soldiers deserting from its ranks, with their weapons, often at the height of a battle, and by Kurdish reluctance generally to fight against fellow Kurds, but the

Kurdish element had to be retained in the Army to counterbalance other factions. For the politically ambitious the Army was the springboard to power, as witnessed by the several military coups and the number of senior officers who became premiers and ministers. Accordingly, the officer corps, which generally fluctuated between 8,000 and 10,000, became obsessed with, and was often splintered by politics. Weakened by frequent political purges over the years, the officer corps was drained of much of its good middle-grade leadership and initiative, so much so that it was a wonder that it was able to mount and sustain the four large military offensives which it did. In fact, military operations in general were surprisingly and reasonably competently organized and directed. The Iraqi Army fought several commendable engagements, but the momentum usually ran down as the mountains were penetrated, the Pesh Merga barred their way and the partisans and tribesmen came into their own.

Another reason for the lack of military success on the part of the Iraqi Army was that the Persian frontier was never really closed to the Kurdish rebels, who were thus able to obtain supplies. Neither Persia, nor Turkey would co-operate fully in the military sense to enable combined operations to be launched that would encircle and crush them. Any partisan movement in the mountains or elsewhere must have a neutral or friendly land frontier, or a stretch of sea coast, to survive. It was also alleged, with some accuracy, that for both the politicians and the Army this was a convenient war, and there was no hurry to end it. For the Army it was the excuse for a high military budget, a large officer corps with many privileges, realistic practice for aircraft pilots and good active service training for the soldiers. For the Government, and political parties and factions, it kept the Army busy, its thoughts from political ambitions and out of Baghdad, but not too far away in case it was required to rush back to the capital to prop up, or topple, a Government.

After a nine-year stalemate it was difficult to see what either the Kurdish rebels or the Government had achieved by struggling on for so long, as the military and political positions were much the same as they had been in 1962, the several Government offensives causing little permanent change. The Kurdish military strength in Iraq had never been really tested, as it had in Turkey and Persia where it had been crushed by systematic and sustained operations by conventional forces. Similar action in Iraq might well have produced a similar result, that is, if taken before the Pesh Merga materialized.

Kurdish rebel strength had been sufficient to hold out independently until it enforced a reluctant peace agreement that amounted to autonomy, the Government giving in for the simple reason that it could not make any military headway. Kurdish political demands for autonomy had long been achieved in fact, as the Government could only partially besiege and blockade, but could not interfere internally.

The abrasive self-reliance of the Kurds, embodied in their proverb, 'The Kurds have no friends,' tended to be detrimental, as did the deductions, drawn by the DPK from the unfortunate Mahabad Republic, that the Kurds had only themselves to rely upon and that it was foolish to depend on others. The Kurds had no powerful friends, nor did they seem to make any serious efforts to win any, whereas if they could have gained the ear, sympathy and help of one or more of the Great Powers, the outcome of the Revolt might have been more favourable to them. It is true that feeble efforts were made to win President Nasser's approbation by the Talabani DPK faction, which were not backed by Mullah Mustafa himself, who held a low opinion of Nasser and wanted little to do with him, but the Kurds suddenly found this platform, which could have meant so much to them, swept away from under their feet by Premier Bazzaz. Hardly any efforts seem to have been made to inform and interest world opinion, the out-of-touch Kurdish exile organizations in Switzerland and Sweden, treated with contempt by Mullah Mustafa, having no material worth exploiting. Visits and speaking tours to foreign states by Mullah Mustafa could have whipped up enthusiasm and raised cash for his Revolt; instead, Mullah Mustafa skulked in his mountains throughout, his external contacts and missions being carried out by others, often badly and unreliably. Efforts to interest the UN were unrewarding, because the Kurds had no powerful ally willing to push their cause before the General Assembly.

Iraqi Governments treated the Kurdish Revolt as a domestic scandal, to be hushed up and dealt with quietly and discreetly, as something that was of no concern to anyone else. They certainly did not welcome meddling outsiders, and tried to keep them out by pretending that all was well in the Kurdish mountains, and that they could not understand what all the fuss was about. In this conspiracy of secrecy the Iraqi Governments were largely successful, as the rest of the world hardly knew of the Kurdish Revolt, apart from the occasional tantalizing glimpse given when some enterprising journalist made his report after visiting the rebels in the field, but these were too few and far between to make any lasting impression. As there was an almost continuous state of tension in the Middle East, while the Revolt was in progress, that dominated the world headlines, interspersed with dramatic events such as the killing of Kassem and the Third Arab–Israeli War, the Kurdish problem came to light only when parts of it were carelessly left uncovered, or when the Government issued boastful communiqués. Alternately, Governments refused all information or put out misleading statements. Had they made no statements at all they would have been more successful in shrouding their Kurdish problem. Journalists, especially foreign ones, had difficulty in obtaining facts, getting to forward areas or seeing for themselves; the censor leaned heavily upon them.

While the attitude of the Iraqi Governments was understandable, that of the rebels was not; they needed the publicity, but took not the slightest advantage of a potentially friendly foreign press. The few Western pressmen who penetrated rebel territory, and saw the 'other side of the Kurdish hill' at first hand, mostly had to scheme hard to get there. Once in rebel territory their welcome was doubtful, as Mullah Mustafa constantly complained that he was misquoted (invariably on trivia), they were mistrusted, their movements restricted and many difficulties deliberately put in their way. Had the publicity techniques of the rebels been better, they would have encouraged a constant stream of journalists to come to see them fighting in the mountains; the resultant reports could hardly have done other than incite admiration, put the Kurdish struggle on the world map, and arouse world opinion.

Whenever insurgency breaks out in whatever part of the world, no matter how remote, quantities of arms appear from mysterious sources, usually provided, or paid for, by states that wish to remain anonymous, but which have an interest in stirring up unrest in that unfortunate country. This was not so in the case of the Kurdish Revolt, and the supply of arms to Mullah Mustafa was sparse. When the Revolt began the tribesmen, and then the partisans, simply had shot-guns and 19th-century firearms. The first modern small arms obtained were those captured from Government sources, such as a few rifles whenever an isolated police post was overrun, or when a small convoy was ambushed, but these probably never amounted to more than a few hundreds in all. By far the greatest number of Kurdish arms obtained were those brought over by Kurdish deserters from the Iraqi armed forces, which totalled several thousands, to which must be added those obtained by trickery and bribery. These were insufficient and many more were required to arm the expanding Pesh Merga.[1]

The Kurdish movement was not a wealthy one in monetary terms, and so large sums of money were not available to purchase arms on the black markets of the Middle East and elsewhere. A certain amount of money was raised for this purpose, which accounts for the possession of a variety of modern weapons especially those of Soviet or Communist origins. Rumours abounded that certain countries might send arms to embarrass CENTO or Arab countries, but there is no positive evidence that the Kurds ever obtained weapons without first having to pay cash for them. Allegations that Israel provided arms and instructors does not seem to have any solid foundation either, although programmes in Arabic beamed from Israel were eagerly listened to because they gave full news treatment on the course of the Revolt and Iraqi Government reaction, but Israeli encouragement seems to have been only verbal.

For the first half of the Revolt the Kurds had nothing heavier than small mortars, and throughout Mullah Mustafa constantly bewailed the fact that he had no artillery with which to bombard Government camps, or anti-aircraft guns to combat air raids. It was only during the last two or three years that he was able to obtain a few guns—and only a few, as in 1970 he had accumulated just over 140 of all types. Ammunition, of course, was another expensive and scarce item, and after having been purchased it had to be carried miles across the mountains by donkey caravan. There was never enough (the Kurds were not noted for good fire discipline), which tended to curtail offensive capability. Mullah Mustafa had to fight his war on a shoestring, but even if he had had ample ammunition it is doubtful whether the ultimate result would have varied, as so much more would simply have been wasted, although certainly Government casualties would have been higher. The Iraqi Air Force will not admit to losing any aircraft through Kurdish rebel activity, but the rebels claim to have brought down at least seventeen. The claim is dubious, but probably they could be credited with destroying up to half a dozen with anti-aircraft fire and damaging others. If they had shot only one down, and they certainly did that, they missed a good

---

[1] One Pesh Merga commander told me on one of my three visits to Kurdish rebel territory that the size of the Pesh Merga was limited to the manner of arms that could be obtained for them.

propaganda trick in not producing, and widely distributing, photographs of the evidence. Iraq was never popular, and such embarrassment would have caused amusement to others.

The story of the Kurdish Revolt is the story of Mullah Mustafa Barzani, the swashbuckling tribal leader, comparatively unlettered, the great survivor who, with his hand firmly on the helm of revolt, rode its stormy course, foiling all attempts to usurp him. With his Barzani tribe, one of the roughest, toughest and most hated in the mountains, as a power base, he expanded his influence and dominance until he became the acknowledged leader of Kurdish nationalism. Standing as he did head and shoulders above all contenders, his reputation, acquired in previous Barzani revolts and in the Mahabad Republic, increased until he became the shining symbol of the Kurdish struggle for recognition and independence. Frequently photographed in Kurdish dress, with bandoliers of ammunition across his chest and carrying a rifle, he was the romantic image of a tribal chief, fighting with his people against a despotic Government, fully sharing all the dangers and hardships. This picture was correct, but there was more to him than that, as apart from being an extrovert personality and a good rabble-rouser[1] who could inspire loyalty, he was an inveterate schemer, full of deviousness, who delighted in political intrigue when he could play one person or faction off against another and then step in to reap any gain or credit from the fracas. He maintained his position on the 'divide and rule' principle, by ensuring that no individual or group gained too much power or prestige

Mullah Mustafa was not a great decision-maker, or a clever, deliberate planner. He meandered along, keeping his own counsel and confiding in no one, relying upon his 'intuition' to tell him when suddenly to take action. Neither could it be claimed that he was a great commander. For many months he had no headquarters from which to conduct the Revolt, but ambled from place to place and so never really knew precisely what was going on at any particular moment. Communications were always poor in Kurdish rebel territory, and thus he was additionally handicapped. Because of poor communications the several Pesh Merga Front commanders had a great degree of initiative and independence. In the field Mullah

---

[1] I once watched him haranguing a group of surly tribesmen who had obviously been detailed to go on some fighting mission they did not like very much. Within seconds of his exhortations to them their expressions changed and within minutes they cheered him before gaily trotting off to carry out whatever task they had objected to such a short time before.

Mustafa tended to lack dash and aggressiveness, and was if anything over-cautious for a partisan leader; he had the 'spider and the fly' complex, and sat endlessly waiting in the 'web' of his mountains for Government 'flies' to enter. He firmly restrained his commanders from venturing down on to the plains; he knew the strengths and weaknesses of his forces, and how to use them to remain secure.

Although Mullah Mustafa quickly gained and held the confidence of the allied tribes, the partisans and the Pesh Merga, he was less sure of the political organization, the DPK, and the civil administration. The younger urbanized Kurds, politically motivated, impatient with old traditions, were anxious to instigate social reforms, but could not do so as the tribal sheikhs, and through them Mullah Mustafa, were at the grass roots of power, and not they. Mullah Mustafa kept the fine balance between the two, and undoubtedly only he could have held the quarrelsome tribes and personalities, with their clashing ideals, together for so long under such strain and adverse conditions. Although not a great commander, Mullah Mustafa was one of the great leaders of the 20th century, being single-minded in his quest and struggle for an autonomous Kurdistan in Iraq, realizing that an independent state would not be viable economically. He was never diverted from his objective, and other matters, such as the Palestine problem, Iraqi confrontation with Persia and Arab rivalries, took a back seat.

One of the great failures brought out in the Kurdish Revolt was the Communist attempt to take it over and dominate it; at each stage, and in every move, they were thwarted and out-manoeuvred by the wily Mullah Mustafa. Initially, the Politburo of the DPK was Communist in composition, and in true Communist style it saw an opportunity to Communize the Kurds in Iraq. The only snag was that the DPK had no support at all in the mountains, and revolt was only feasible with tribal backing, so Mullah Mustafa, having ample grass roots support, was acknowledged by the DPK as the leader, it meaning to oust him when he was of no further use. Mullah Mustafa remained the nominal and reluctant Chairman of the DPK, but Jalal Talabani rose to become the leader of the dissident faction of the DPK, attempting to carve out an independent DPK sector as a preliminary to expanding it as an instrument to carry out the ultimate Communist aim. Talabani was outwitted by Mullah Mustafa, who forced him into the open on to the Government side. Eleven years in the Soviet Union had not converted Mullah Mustafa to Communism, but it had given him a good insight into how it operated, and so he was able to combat its insidious techniques.

Meanwhile, after expelling Talabani and his political colleagues, Mullah Mustafa set about purging the DPK of all not loyal to himself and reshaping it, placing his own nominees on all decision-making committees. Although some of the younger urbanized Kurds, who held minor positions in the DPK and the civil administration, were discontented, they held their peace because Mullah Mustafa had absolute control of the rebel military forces, and had already shown he would not hesitate to march his Pesh Merga against any faction that criticized his leadership, tried to usurp him, or attempted to form dissident splinter groups. Talabani and his colleagues possessed good organizing ability and intense drive but, having nothing to organize, their talents were applied to intrigue and so were dissipated in unsuccessful rivalry against Mullah Mustafa. Had Talabani gained control of the Revolt the outcome might have been different, with an internal struggle developing as the DPK forced socialism on the unwilling mountain Kurds, in the effort to squeeze them into a Communist mould, while at the same time keeping Government forces at bay. When it took the field in the spring of 1962, Mullah Mustafa would not allow the DPK to enter his area, and so it was forced to carve one out for itself. This was the DPK sector, which soon was better organized than that of Mullah Mustafa. Talabani also showed a degree of military aptitude, and his Pesh Merga, some 630 only, caused the Government forces more trouble than did the 15,000 under Mullah Mustafa. An outstanding example of their ability was shown at the battle for the Ruwandiz Gorge, that lasted from June to August 1963, which was almost entirely a DPK action.

Having attained the principle of Kurdish autonomy within Iraq, the Kurds are now chafing at the slow implementation of its conditions, but they should have become used by now to such Iraqi delaying tactics. Previous Governments have shown that they never had any intention, despite what they may have said on occasions, of granting the Kurds any more political freedom than they could prevent the Kurds from taking; they played for time in endless talks and conferences, and dallied with such opaque expressions as 'decentralization' and 'Kurdish national rights within the Iraqi nation'. What the Kurds could not get from a succession of weak Governments, they will be unlikely to obtain from stronger ones, magnanimity not being a common trait in the Middle East. Despite promises the present

April–June: Mullah Mustafa launches a spring offensive, mainly against hostile tribes.

20th April: Amnesty refused by Kurds.

Mullah Mustafa issues a manifesto.

June–October: Pesh Merga and partisans organized in rebel territory.

9th July: Iraqi aircraft bomb Turkish frontier posts by mistake.

July: Unofficial peace-feelers by Sheikh Ahmed Barzani.

HQ of 1st Infantry Division moves up north to Mosul.

16th August: Turks shoot down an Iraqi aircraft.

30th August: Kurdish attempt to blow up oil pipeline.

10th October: British oil technician captured by Kurds (another on 26th November 1963).

10th January: Kassem offers the Kurdish rebels a second amnesty.

January: Meetings between Kurds and Baathists.

8th February: Free Officers Movement coup—Kassem killed—succeeded by Abdul Salem Aref.

Chapter 5

1963

February: Statements by Committee for the Defence of the Kurdish People's Rights.

Negotiations between Kurdish Rebels and Iraqi Government.

May: Mongolian People's Republic asks UN to put Kurdish question before the General Assembly (withdrawn in September).

Iraq Government in difficulties.

Negotiations with Kurds run into difficulties.

10th June: Second offensive begins (lasts until October).

Syrian brigade already in Iraq.

17th June: Battle for the Ruwandiz Gorge begins (lasts until 12th August).

Oil installations near Kirkuk blown up.

22nd June: Explosions in Baghdad army camps.

30th June: Syrian aircraft reported flying with Iraqi Air Force.

30th July: Talks between Iraqi Government and Kurdish Rebels (lasting until 11th August).

1st August: Zibar occupied by Government troops.

4th August: Barzan occupied by Government troops.

10th August: Zakho occupied by Government troops.

11th August: Kurdish demands rejected by Iraqi Government.

August: Turkish and Persian plans for invading Iraq to attack Kurds revealed.

September: DPK HQ at Chami-Razan evacuated.

October: Government military units withdraw to Baghdad.

November: Kurdish rebels occupy territory evacuated by Government troops.

Internal Baathist power struggle.

18th November: Coup against Baathists—street fighting in Baghdad —Baathist National Guard militia crushed.

20th November: Taher Yahya forms Government.

1964

January: Cease-fire negotiations between Kurdish rebels and Government begin.

10th February: President Aref announces a cease-fire.

Chapter 6

1964

12th February: President Aref announces a cease-fire.

March: Friction between Mullah Mustafa and the DPK.

Jalal Talabani, of the DPK, visits President Nasser.

3rd May: New provisional constitution announced, guaranteeing Kurdish national rights within Iraqi national unity.

May: Mullah Mustafa's Pesh Merga push south into the DPK sector.

5th June: Talks between Mullah Mustafa and Premier Taher Yahya.

18th June: New Government formed by Taher Yahya.

14th July: Formation of Iraqi Arab Socialist Union, to incorporate all legal political parties—DPK excluded.

Banks and some commercial concerns nationalized.

July: Mullah Mustafa's Pesh Merga forces DPK element out into Persia.

Attempt by reinforced DPK to re-enter Iraq defeated by Barzanis.

Mullah Mustafa convenes DPK Congress at Raniya.

5th September: Unsuccessful Sadi plot against the Government.

186

September: Mullah Mustafa holds a Kurdish Congress at Raniya.
4th October: Kurdish rebel administration established.
11th October: Mullah Mustafa sends fresh demands to the Government.
October: Clashes between Government troops and Kurdish rebels.
14th November: New Government formed by Taher Yahya.
December: Secret Baathist Congress.

1965

6th January: Abolition of martial law in Iraq.
February: Mullah Mustafa makes last peace efforts.
April–September: Third offensive by Government troops.
May–June: Reconciliation between Mullah Mustafa and DPK faction.
June: Plots against the Iraqi Government.
July: Rikabi incident.
August: Riots in streets of Baghdad.
5th September: Government formed by Aref Abdul Razzak.
15th September: Unsuccessful coup by Razzak.
21st September: Government formed by Abdul Rahman al-Bazzaz, a civilian.

Chapter 7

1965

26th October: President Nasser supports Iraqi Government against the Kurdish rebels.

1966

January: Government winter offensive against Panjwin area.
18th February: Mullah Mustafa sends memorandum to UN.
February: Mullah Mustafa clashes with Talabani, who flees from DPK sector.
13th April: Death of President Abdul Salem Aref—succeeded by Abdul Rahman Aref, his elder brother.
17th April: Bazzaz forms a new Government.
4th May: Fourth offensive begins (lasts only until the end of the month).
11th–12th May: Battle of Mount Handrin.

June: Peace talks between the Government and the Kurdish rebels.
29th June: Premier Bazzaz announces his Twelve Point Programme for the Kurds.
30th June: Attempted Razzak coup.
6th August: Premier Bazzaz resigns.
9th August: Naji Taleb forms a Government.
October: President Aref visits Mullah Mustafa in Kurdish territory. Mullah Mustafa holds a Kurdish conference.

1967

10th May: President Aref assumes post of Premier.
5th–10th June: Third Arab–Israel War (Six Day War).
10th July: Taher Yahya forms a Government.
3rd December: Kurdish language newspaper suspended.
Reported attempt to assassinate Jalal Talabani.
Sabotage in the Kirkuk oil installations.

Chapter 8

1968

February: Kurds prevent French arms being sent to Iraq.
12th–13th April: Kurdish rebels attack Army patrol near Arbil.
6th July: Last Kurdish minister resigns from Yahya Government.
12th July: Premier Yahya resigns (forms another Government on the 16th).
17th July: Baathist coup led by General Bakr—President Aref sent into exile.
19th July: Colonel Abdul Razzak al-Nayef forms a Government.
31st July: President Bakr assumes post of Premier.
3rd August: Revolutionary Command Council announces it will settle the Kurdish problem on the Twelve Point Programme.
October: Fighting between Mullah Mustafa and Jalal Talabani—Government troops assist Talabani.
18th November: Mullah Mustafa protests to the UN, alleging the Government is practising genocide.

1969

3rd January: Government launches a military offensive that takes Kala-Diza and Panjwin (lasts for three weeks only).

1st March: Mullah Mustafa launches a counter-offensive—regains territory.

Sabotage in the Kirkuk oil installations.

15th March: Iraqi brigade serving in Syria.

9th April: Unsuccessful attempt to assassinate Mullah Mustafa.

20th April: Persian troops reported massing near Iraqi border.

June: Secret talks between representatives of the Bakr Government and Mullah Mustafa in Beirut.

August (last week): Government launches a military offensive against the Kurdish rebels (lasting for three weeks).

21st–22nd September: Pesh Merga makes successful night attack on Army camp near Dukan.

October: Government concessions to the Kurds.

December: Contact made between President Bakr and Mullah Mustafa.

1970

20th January: Unsuccessful plot against the Government.

24th January: Bakr Government announces it will support the Twelve Point Programme.

January: Negotiations between the Bakr Government and the Kurdish rebels begin.

11th March: Armistice agreement signed, and 15-point peace settlement with the Kurds announced.

18th March: Nine-man committee formed to implement peace settlement.

3rd July: Mullah Mustafa holds Kurdish Conference.

16th July: New provisional constitution promulgated incorporating some Kurdish demands.

16th October: Plebiscite for Kirkuk postponed indefinitely.

INDEX

The following words are not included in the Index, as they are on a majority of the pages:

Barzani, Mulla Mustafa;   DPK Iraq(i)(s)   Kurd(ishs(s)
Persia(n)(s)   Pesh Merga

Said, Nuri, 26, 39, 42, 44, 45, 47, 58–62, 130
Said, Sheikh, 27
Sakalli, Fathi, Brigadier, 103, 116
Saladin, 15
Saladin Force, 106, 145, 147, 152
Sallal, Field Marshal, 97
Sanandaj, 54
Saqquiz, 40, 43, 53, 54, 121
Sarband, Mount, 87
Sarbaz, 52
Sardasht, 40, 53, 54, 121
Sardashy-Zanjan Line, 40, 51–3
Sar Merga, 85
Saudi Arabia(n), 141
Secretary-General—see UN
Secretary-General (Bureau of Kurdistan), 158
Sevres, Treaty of, 20
Shah Mohammed Raza Pahlavi, 40
Shah Reza, 30, 31, 39, 40, 42, 83, 94, 166
Shali, Abdul Fattah, al-, 147
Shaklawa (tribe), 72
Shammar (tribe), 66, 67
Shatt-al-Arab, 70, 153, 163, 166
Shawaf, Colonel, 66, 67
Shias, 33, 63, 128, 129
Shikak (tribe), 2p, 30, 33, 53–5
Shirzada, Ihsan, 148, 149
Showais, Nuri Sadik, 61
Shukri, Shaker Mohammed, Major-General, 136, 137, 141
Sidki, Bakr, General, 25, 26
Simel, 25
Simko Revolts, 20, 30
Sinjar, 58
Soviet Ambassador, 42
Soviet Defence Minister, 147
Soviet Union, 11, 12, 20, 26, 28, 29, 31, 32, 34, 38–43, 48–58, 60, 62–4, 69, 72, 86–9, 92, 101, 102, 108, 110, 112, 127, 135, 141, 144, 147, 154, 166, 167, 173, 175
Sovereignty Council, 80
Stalingrad(battle of), 43
Suez, 61
Suleimaniya, 21, 25, 41, 43–5, 58, 59, 71, 72, 75, 76, 79, 87, 91, 92, 100, 101, 103, 106, 109, 112, 114, 121, 125, 126, 137, 145, 151, 156
Sunnis, 33, 63
Surehis, 49, 69, 83

Sweden, 171
Switzerland, 171
Syria(n)(s), 20, 29, 31, 32, 34, 39, 45, 61, 66, 67, 69, 80, 86, 90, 92, 93, 95, 101–4, 113, 114, 118, 121, 143, 147, 153, 154, 167
Syrian Air Force, 108
Syrian Government, 80, 103, 108, 167
Syrian Kurds, 80

T-34s (tanks), 57, 91, 110
T-54s (tanks, 154
T-55s (tanks), 154
Taakhi, al-, 144
Tabriz, 20, 49, 55
Tafar, Sheikh, 31
Takrit, 15
Takriti, Hardan, Brigadier, 114, 122, 149
Takrit, Saddam Hussein, 158, 159
Talabani, Hassan 66, 135, 139, 149
Talabani, Jelal, 61, 78, 87, 96, 99, 100, 102, 108, 117–22, 127, 134, 139, 140, 142, 145, 147, 150–2, 155, 158, 159, 163, 168, 171, 176
Taleb, Naji, 141, 142
Talili (tribe), 57
Talin, 31
Teheran, 19, 29, 30, 39, 40, 43, 54, 55, 118–21, 134, 135, 157
Tel Aviv, 143
Tigris, River, 15
Timur, Amir (Tamerlane), 15
Tobacco, 33
Trans-Jordan, 59
Treaty (of 1937), 153
Tripartite Agreement (of 1926), 22, 118
Tripartite Treaty (of 1941), 40, 51
TU-16s (aircraft), 143
Tudeh Party, 42, 54, 94
Turk(ey)(ish), 11, 13, 15–23, 25–30, 32–5, 43–4, 51, 56, 57, 59, 69–71, 75, 76, 81, 82, 87, 90, 93, 94, 126, 134, 140
Turkish Air Force, 28
Turkish Army, 27–9, 70, 93
Turkish Democratic Party, 70, 161, 164, 165, 167, 170, 177, 178
Turkish Empire, 11
Turkish Government, 27–9, 70, 93, 112, 164
Turkish Kurds, 41